W9-AAK-318

# GLADIATORS

## FIGHTING TO THE DEATH IN ANCIENT ROME

M. C. Bishop

**CASEMATE**

*Oxford & Philadelphia*

Published in Great Britain and
the United States of America in 2017 by
CASEMATE PUBLISHERS
The Old Music Hall, 106–108 Cowley Road, Oxford OX4 1JE, UK
1950 Lawrence Road, Havertown, PA 19083, USA

© Casemate Publishers 2017

Paperback Edition: ISBN 978-1-61200-513-3
Digital Edition: ISBN 978-1-61200-514-0 (epub)

All rights reserved. No part of this book may be reproduced or transmitted in
any form or by any means, electronic or mechanical including photocopying,
recording or by any information storage and retrieval system, without
permission from the publisher in writing.

A CIP record for this book is available from the British Library


Printed in the Czech Republic by FINIDR, s.r.o.
Typeset in India by Lapiz Digital Services, Chennai

For a complete list of Casemate titles, please contact:

CASEMATE PUBLISHERS (UK)
Telephone (01865) 241249
Email: casemate-uk@casematepublishers.co.uk
www.casematepublishers.co.uk

CASEMATE PUBLISHERS (US)
Telephone (610) 853-9131
Fax (610) 853-9146
Email: casemate@casematepublishers.com
www.casematepublishers.com

# CONTENTS

| | |
|---|---|
| **275 BC** | Manius Curius Dentatus first displays elephants in a triumph in Rome (Italy)  · |
| **264 BC** | First recorded public gladiatorial combat in the Forum Boarium |
| **216 BC** | First gladiatorial combat staged in the Forum Romanum |
| **206 BC** | Scipio Africanus holds games for his father and uncle at New Carthage (Spain) |
| **186 BC** | Marcus Fulvius Nobilior stages first wild beast hunt in Rome |
| **167 BC** | Elephants first used to trample Roman army deserters |
| **105 BC** | Publius Rutilius Rufus turns to gladiatorial instructors to train Roman legionaries |
| **80 BC** | Stone amphitheatre built at Pompeii (Italy) |
| **73–71 BC** | Revolt of Spartacus |
| **52 BC** | First timber amphitheatre recorded |
| **46 BC** | Caesar holds games which include a *naumachia* (sham naval battle) on the Campus Martius |
| **29 BC** | First stone amphitheatre built in Rome |
| **2 BC** | Augustus stages a *naumachia* across the Tiber |
| **AD 21** | Revolt of Florus and Sacrovir in Gaul |
| **AD 52** | Claudius stages a *naumachia* on the Fucine Lake |
| **AD 57** | Nero holds games including a *naumachia* in his new wooden amphitheatre |
| **AD 59** | Riot at Pompeii; games in the amphitheatre there banned for ten years |
| **AD 62** | Earthquake at Pompeii and the ban on games is lifted |
| **AD 70** | (approximately) Timber amphitheatre built at London (UK) |

| **AD 72** | Flavian Amphitheatre (Colosseum) inaugurated |
| **AD 75** | Stone amphitheatre built at the legionary fortress of Caerleon (UK) |
| **AD 79** | Amphitheatre at Pompeii buried by the eruption of Vesuvius |
| **AD 158** | Galen starts work on gladiators |
| **AD 177** | Limit on expenditure on gladiatorial games |
| **AD 200** | Septimius Severus bans female gladiators |
| **AD 248** | Philip the Arab's Secular Games |
| **AD 404** | Gladiatorial games supposedly banned in Rome by Honorius |
| **AD 1823** | Amphitheatre at Pompeii rediscovered |
| **AD 1864** | Gladiatorial barracks at Pompeii excavated |
| **AD 1872** | *Pollice Verso* painted by Jean-Léon Gérôme |
| **AD 1933** | James Leslie Mitchell (alias Lewis Grassic Gibbon) publishes his *Spartacus* novel |
| **AD 1951** | Howard Fast publishes his *Spartacus* novel |
| **AD 1960** | Stanley Kubrick's *Spartacus* released |
| **AD 2000** | Ridley Scott's movie *Gladiator* released |

# TECHNICAL GLOSSARY

THERE ARE A NUMBER OF LATIN WORDS that occur repeatedly in the following. Rather than try to find English equivalents, it seems much easier to retain the original terms.

| | |
|---|---|
| *aedile (aedilis)* | magistrate responsible for organising *munera* |
| *amphitheatrum* | amphitheatre |
| *armatura* | weapons drill; type of gladiator or style of fighting |
| *auctoratus* | a free man who fights as a gladiator |
| *balteus* | broad metal belt worn by gladiators |
| *bestiarius* | animal fighter |
| *bustuarii* | early nickname for gladiators ('cremation-pit boys') |
| *caesim* | cutting or chopping with a sword |
| *cena libera* | public meal for gladiators the evening before a fight |
| *censor* | magistrate responsible for the census and public morality |
| *dictata* | 'the rules', a formulaic series of offensive and defensive moves |
| *doctor* | trainer |

| | |
|---|---|
| *editor* | overall organiser of a *munus* |
| *gladius* | sword (generally used of the short sword) |
| *lanista* | owner or manager of a *ludus* |
| *libellus* | booklet with details of the gladiator pairings |
| *ludus* | gladiatorial school |
| *ludi* | gladiatorial games |
| *missio* | dismissal alive after a combat |
| *munus* | gladiatorial games |
| *naumachia* | mock naval battle |
| *noxii* | condemned men and prisoners of war sentenced to the arena |
| *palus* stake | (as high as a person) against which a gladiator trained |
| *parmularii* | small-shield fighters (and their followers) |
| *pollice verso* | gesture with the thumb to indicate death or survival |
| *pompa* | procession before games begin |
| *prolusio* | prologue to gladiatorial combat fought with dummy weapons |
| *primus palus* | top-ranking gladiator in a *ludus* |
| *probatio armorum* | inspection of weaponry before combat |
| *pugio* | dagger |
| *punctim* | stabbing with a sword (or dagger) |
| *rudis* | double-weight wooden sword used for training, awarded upon retirement |
| *sacramentum gladiatorum* | oath taken by gladiators |
| *scutarii* | big-shield fighters (and their followers) |
| *scutum* | shield |
| *spectacula* | gladiatorial show; old name for amphitheatre |

| | |
|---|---|
| *subligaculum* | loin cloth or breech cloth worn by gladiators |
| *summa rudis* | umpire |
| *tiro* | recruit, greenhorn |
| *velaria* | awning made up of many *vela* (see *velum*) |
| *velum* | one panel of the *velaria*; plural *vela* |
| *venator* | hunter |
| *veteranus* | experienced gladiator |
| *vomitoria* | exits from an amphitheatre |

# CHAPTER 1

## INTRODUCTION

*History does not permit peoples to be judged
by a simple good or bad mark.*

Michael Grant, *Gladiators*

## Who was a gladiator?

After all, what has Norbanus ever done for us? He produced some
decayed twopenny-halfpenny gladiators, who would have fallen flat
if you breathed on them; I have seen better ruffians turned in to fight
the wild beasts. He shed the blood of some mounted infantry that
might have come off a lamp; dunghill cocks you would have called
them: one a spavined mule, the other bandylegged, and the holder
of the bye, just one corpse instead of another, and hamstrung. One
man, a Thracian, had some stuffing, but he too fought according to
the rule of the schools. In short, they were all flogged afterwards.
How the great crowd roared at them, 'Lay it on!' They were mere
runaways, to be sure. 'Still,' says Norbanus, 'I did give you a treat.'
Yes, and I clap my hands at you. Reckon it up, and I give you more
than I got. One good turn deserves another.

–Petronius, *Satyricon* 45

Reading this passage, from one of the first prose novels in the
western world, is one way to judge the distance between us and

the people of Rome. The familiarity of the speaker with what he is describing – entertainment provided by men fighting for their lives – helps render what he is describing everyday and unsurprising. His tone is that of the football pundit on the couch, which is the thing that strikes an uncomfortable familiarity for us too, because on one level, we can understand this: the team was mostly useless, although the Thracian showed some gumption, and the crowd were not impressed either; the gladiators did not really earn their applause.

The Latin word *gladiator* originally meant 'sword-fighter', deriving from *gladius*, which meant any sort of sword. Over time, the word *gladius* was often associated with the classic short sword wielded by Roman legionaries, often known as the *gladius Hispaniensis* ('Spanish sword') and this is indeed what we find many early gladiators using. However, the label gladiator was extended to cover a range of types of performance artists who competed in the life-and-death struggles of the arena, many of them never even using swords. One of the most famous types of gladiator – not least because one was played by Woody Strode in Stanley Kubrick's *Spartacus* – was the *retiarius* or 'net-man'. Armed with his weighted net and trident (both possibly modelled on the equipment of fishermen), he would attempt to trip or engulf his opponent with his net, whilst keeping him at a distance (and finally dealing a deadly blow) with his trident. There were variants on the type – one who used a lasso instead of a net and one who stood on a platform and threw stones – but there was little doubt in the minds of the Romans that a *retiarius*, despite his lack of a sword, was a gladiator.

Men who fought each other were not the only type of gladiator. Those who fought wild animals (*bestiarii*) or participated in hunts in the arena (*venatores*) were also included, to judge from the fact that they had their own training school. There are even sculpted reliefs showing men equipped as gladiators locked in combat with big cats, so there is no doubt that this was seen as 'gladiatorial' by the Romans themselves. It is sometimes difficult for us to distinguish between *bestiarii* and *venatores* and it is by no means clear that the Romans were either certain or consistent in making that distinction.

There were also men who fought against each other who were not gladiators. Usually condemned criminals or prisoners of war, they were given none of the training or privileges of gladiators, but instead were expected to fight enthusiastically, usually in recreations of great battles from the past (although normally not major Roman defeats like the Battles of Caudine Forks, Cannae, or Trasimene, for fairly obvious reasons). These might be land battles, complete with scenery, or even (from the time of Julius Caesar onwards) naval engagements known as *naumachia*. Alongside those condemned to play a part in a gruesome piece of historical re-enactment, there were also those sentenced to be killed *ad bestias*. Being torn apart by wild animals was yet another form of entertainment provided for the crowd, rendered all too familiar by tales of Christian martyrs forced to die in this way. All of these unfortunates had just one thing in common: nobody was looking for the skill or finesse of the gladiator, they were just there to be slaughtered.

Finally there were gladiators who provided light relief, rather than gory scenes of death, and these included the *paegnarii* (who fought each other with sticks) or the *andabatae*, who duelled (or, rather, attempted to do so) in helmets with no eye holes.

All of these categories of more-or-less deadly entertainment were to be found in what we call the 'games' but Romans referred to as *munera*. A *munus* was another word whose meaning evolved over time. It started out as an obligation or duty, usually on the part of a politician, to provide a service. This developed from providing funeral games in honour of a notable deceased figure into putting on entertainment for the masses. Finally, *munera* became synonymous with the games and interchangeable with the word *ludi* (a *ludus* was a gladiatorial training school, but *ludi* in the plural were always games). They became staggeringly expensive to stage, could last for weeks and often imposed a logistical strain on the entire Roman Empire just to provide entertainment in the capital. However, the games were an integral and pervasive aspect of Roman life that inevitably impinges on our perception of the people and their time: who can think of Rome without thinking of gladiators?

# The fascination of gladiators

What is it about gladiators that fascinates us still? The Romans experienced a perplexing ambivalence towards them, at once once fascinated and revolted by gladiators. The fact that some free men (and even women) chose to sign up for the life demonstrates just how powerful the pull of the arena could be for some. In the most extreme cases, an emperor might choose to join in. However, whilst it was not thought acceptable for an emperor to fight as a gladiator, there seemed to be no objection to training in one of the particular variants of gladiatorial combat. As we shall see, it was thought to be a clear benefit that Roman soldiers were trained in this way. The shame all seems to have come from being seen to compete in public.

Modern 'civilised' people like to think that they have risen above this sort of thing and that watching large numbers of people being killed is not something we would do. Yet we are quite content to watch it in the cinema or on television. One famous study from 1976 estimated that, by the time they graduated from high school, the average American child had seen 13,000 simulated deaths on television. Other studies noted that violence in prime-time dramas was often glamorised, whilst in children's cartoons it was trivialised. In 2012, another study (by an online undertaker) was published, revealing that in 2011 a single week's viewing of 40 monitored programmes produced 132 simulated dead human bodies.

Of course, we all know these are not real dead bodies and that the actors get up again and go home at the end of a day's shoot. But are we not a little bit inured to the spectacle of death and just ever so slightly intrigued by the deaths of gladiators, mostly anonymised behind their large, visored helmets? Is it part of the fascination of gladiators that we identify to some extent with those ancient Roman audiences? In other words, are we closer to the crowd attending a gladiatorial contest than we might care to admit?

# Modern histories

We have come a long way from when Michael Grant's *Gladiators* was about the only popular book available on the subject. Now there are many, but still comparatively few that systematically examine the history of gladiatorial combat from its inception to its end. It is important to consider the historical development of the gladiatorial games, because the nature of the games changed over time, gradually evolving from a funeral rite under the early Republic (509 to 264 BC), through a political tool for the manipulation of the masses under the mid- and later Republic (264 to 27 BC) and into pure entertainment in the Imperial (27 BC to AD 296) and Late Roman (AD 296 to 410) periods.

Thus a historical framework lies at the core of what follows, with digressions to examine the equipment and venues of the gladiatorial games, as well as the everyday life of gladiators and what actually happened in the arena. There is much that such a narrative approach can bring to the fore, such as the fact that the Samnite and Gaul gladiator types were only in use during the Republican period, so they were active for less than half of the period during which we know that gladiatorial combat was popular. Similarly, the *retiarius* was not introduced until the early Imperial period. More crucially, it can mirror the changes in Roman society as they are reflected in the taste for watching men (and women) kill each other and wild animals in a variety of innovative ways.

Between 2000 and 2001, an exhibition of gladiatorial material was held first in Hamburg in February to June 2000, in Speyer in July to October 2000 and then in the British Museum from October 2000 to January 2001, the accompanying catalogue for which was published as *Gladiators and Caesars*. In 2002, the exhibition *Gladiatoren in Ephesos: Tod am Nachmittag* ('*Gladiators in Ephesus: Death in the Afternoon*') was mounted, bringing details of the Ephesus gladiator cemetery to the general public for the first time, at the same time placing the results in the wider context of gladiatorial combat. Such events inevitably have a far-reaching effect and inspire both more reading and more writing about gladiators. For all that is known, there is still much to find out, and this book will hopefully provide both a glimpse of the former and hint at the latter.

# CHAPTER 2

# ORIGINS

*The Gladiators [sic] Art was Infamous for its Barbarity and Cruelty, involving Men in Murder and Bloodshed.*

Thomas Bingham

## Funeral games

IT MAY BE SURPRISING TO LEARN that the origins of gladiatorial combat can be seen as early as Homer's *Iliad* with its account of the funeral games following the death of Patroclus. Immediately before Achilles lights his companion's funeral pyre, he executes twelve Trojan captives. Next day, the Trojans embark on a series of games, including boxing, wrestling, archery and chariot racing. That passage thereby combines human sacrifice and sporting contest in the context of marking a death and, as such, is seen by many as providing a context for the Roman adoption of gladiatorial combat.

Similarly, there are historical instances recorded of prisoners of war being executed en masse. Greek and Carthaginian prisoners were stoned to death by the Etruscans (a people who lived to the north of Rome) at Caere (Cerveteri, Italy) in the 6th century BC. Then, in 358 BC, more than 300 Roman prisoners of war were executed in the forum at Tarchuna (Tarquinia in Italy), again by the Etruscans. These grisly events provide an association between victory and mass killings, but those survivors taken prisoner could find their agony prolonged when they were forced to fight each other.

The Christian writer Tertullian provided his own interpretation of this, with the benefit of several hundred years of hindsight and through the lens of his particular theological perspective:

> The ancients thought that by this sort of spectacle they rendered a service to the dead, after they had tempered it with a more cultured form of cruelty. For of old, in the belief that the souls of the dead are propitiated with human blood, they used at funerals to sacrifice captives or slaves of poor quality whom they bought. Afterwards it seemed good to obscure their impiety by making it a pleasure. So after the persons procured had been trained in such arms as they then had and as best they might – their training was to learn to be killed! – they then did them to death on the appointed funeral day at the tombs. So they found comfort for death in murder. This is the origin of the *munus*. (Tertullian, *On Spectacles* 12)

## The first gladiators

It is entirely appropriate to stress that most of our source material about the origins of gladiatorial combat is not contemporary with those distant origins. Writers such as Nicolaus of Damascus, Livy and Silius Italicus were working in the late 1st century BC or 1st century AD and thus were writing up to three centuries after the events they were describing. Livy's history of Rome, known as *Ab Urbe Condita* (*From the City's Foundation*) began from the traditional (and probably spurious) date of 753 BC, but it is worth remembering that historical writing did not actually begin in the classical world until Herodotus, a Greek from Halicarnassus, produced his *Historia* in the 5th century BC. So a lot of Rome's early 'history' was, technically, prehistory and, for the most part, legendary. Such legends will have been passed on by word of mouth, songs learned by one generation and bequeathed to the next, but these are not the same as documented fact. All of this means that it is sometimes necessary to distinguish between what the Romans who were writing *thought* happened in the past and what actually occurred. A little caution is always healthy.

The Greek writer Athenaeus (middle of the 2nd century AD) preserved a report by the above-mentioned Nicolaus of Damascus (second half of the 1st century BC) which included the observation that gladiatorial games were inherited by the Romans from the Etruscans (who, unlike most of Italy, did not speak a language derived from Indo-European). Even if Nicolaus was correct (and some scholars feel that there is good reason to doubt it), it is by no means certain that the path for the idea of gladiatorial combat from the Etruscans to the Romans was a direct one, despite the Romans believing that they had been ruled by the Etruscans. After all, it was part of their tradition that they cast out their Etruscan rulers, the Tarquins, and formed the Republic in 509 BC.

Overlooking the literary sources for the time being, the identification of the Etruscans as the originators of gladiatorial games depends upon a number of observations that are not necessarily linked. First there are frescoes from Etruscan tombs which show combat between two warriors. Single combat between important warriors featured in the *Iliad* too, and there is no obvious reason why the pairs of figures in the wall paintings must be interpreted as men fighting to the death in funerary games. Second is the spectral figure of Charun or Dis Pater, an Etruscan deity who appeared in Roman contexts as an arena assistant in costume, whose job was to kill off any losers who might not be quite dead enough with a large mallet. Charun is shown, complete with blue-grey skin and large hammer, on a 4th-century BC fresco from a tomb at Vulci (Italy) depicting the killing of prisoners during the Trojan War. Third is the Latin term for the gladiatorial trainer, *lanista*, a word that Isidore of

Seville (writing in the 6th/7th century AD) thought dated back to the Etruscans. The Romans loved the sort of word archaeology that is etymology, but we now know that they were hopeless at it and frequently got the origins of Latin words very wrong. Was the supposed Etruscan origin of *lanista* projected backwards because the Romans 'knew' how the games began? Did the whole idea of dressing up as Charun also ultimately derive from the traditional notion of an Etruscan origin for gladiatorial games? The Romans were more than a little fascinated by the Etruscans, as the Emperor Claudius' studies showed (he was allegedly the last person able to read their language).

The Etruscan origin hypothesis was not the only one available, however. Livy, writing more than two centuries later when describing the aftermath of the Roman war in Samnium in 308 BC, noted that

> the Campanians, in consequence of their pride and in hatred of the Samnites, equipped after this fashion the gladiators who furnished them entertainment at their feasts, and bestowed on them the name of Samnites. (Livy 9.40.17–18)

The Campanians lived to the south of Rome, in the area around the Bay of Naples. This is the region that saw some of the first stone amphitheatres, at Capua and Pompeii, although whether this is significant is unclear.

The Latin term for men who fought around funerary pyres in this way (probably half-joking – Cicero used it in a speech to mock an opponent) was *bustuarii* or 'cremation-pit boys' (a *bustum* was a type of cremation pyre built over a pit where the remains rather neatly collapsed into the pit once well alight).

Suetonius, famous for his racy biographies of the first few emperors, believed that the first gladiatorial games dated back to the time of Lucius Tarquinius Priscus (late 7th to early 6th centuries BC), one of the legendary Etruscan rulers of early Rome. Gaius Maenius, the censor in 338 BC (whose responsibilities included public morality and maintaining the census), was said to have enlarged the seating capacity in the Forum for spectators of gladiatorial shows. In so doing, he gave his name to the seating later used in amphitheatres: *maeniana*. However, we are told by several sources (none of them contemporary, unfortunately), that the first Roman gladiatorial combat ever staged was held in 264 BC, when Decimus Junius Brutus arranged one to commemorate his recently deceased father. Livy, whose work survives only as a summary at this point, simply notes that

> Decimus Junius Brutus was the first to give a gladiatorial exhibition, in honour of his dead father (Livy 16 summary)

but other authors give us more detail. Valerius Maximus, for instance, writing in the first half of the 1st century AD, observed that

> gladiatorial games were first presented in Rome in the Forum Boarium, during the consulships of Appius Claudius and Quintus Fulvius. They were provided by Marcus and Decimus, sons of Brutus Pera, honouring their father's ashes with a funerary memorial. (Valerius Maximus 2.4.7)

Whilst it was not strictly history, the Romans were already keeping lists of their consuls (the *Fasti Consulares*) at this period, sometimes annotating them with notable contemporary events, so it is not wholly implausible that Livy may have had access to these records. More detail is then provided by the 4th-century AD writer Ausonius, although its authenticity is uncertain:

> The first three fights were of Thracians in three pairs, offered by the sons of Junius at the tomb of their father (Ausonius, *Riddle of the Number Three* 36–7)

Whether gladiatorial combat did indeed suddenly appear in the Roman world like this is questionable, but the fact that the tradition is preserved in the sources at least gives us an idea of how far back it was that it began to be common. One interesting suggestion that has been made is that 264 BC actually marked the first time that gladiatorial combat was provided as a public spectacle in Rome, having previously been confined to private audiences at feasts and funerals.

By 216 BC, the venue had shifted:

> In honour of Marcus Aemilius Lepidus, who had been consul twice and augur, his three sons, Lucius, Marcus, and Quintus, gave funeral games for three days and showed twenty-two pairs of gladiators in the Forum [Romanum]. (Livy 23.30.15)

The year is significant, for the games followed soon after the major Roman defeat at Cannae, when a reported 70,000 Romans were massacred by Hannibal's forces. It has been suggested that the development of gladiatorial shows as public entertainment can be traced back to the effects of this traumatic defeat, with magistrates incorporating ever more prisoners of war into the games to produce a feel-good factor amongst the public.

The link had now been made between funeral rite, public entertainment and politics, and this was to have profound consequences in the years to come. The phenomenon went from strength to strength and the number of pairs of gladiators increased every time, as each noble family tried to outdo their rivals. In 200 BC, 25 pairs of gladiators fought at the funeral of Marcus Valerius Laevinus, whilst in 183 BC, 60 pairs were matched to mark the death of Publius Licinius Crassus, together with a distribution of meat, funeral games and a banquet. The association of gifts of food with the games is interesting as it reoccurs in later periods. All of these were staged in the Forum Romanum, at the heart of Roman political life, and this was to remain the principal venue for such fights until the development of amphitheatres in Rome in the later 1st century BC. It has even been observed that the arena of the amphitheatre at Pompeii would fit neatly within the available open space of the

Forum Romanum, so it may be that the way in which it was set up for gladiatorial fights inspired amphitheatre development in some way.

Gladiatorial combat was not confined to Rome. In 206 BC, Scipio Africanus commemorated his deceased uncle and father whilst based at New Carthage in Spain with his army. There was a rather unusual twist to it, if Livy is to be believed:

> The exhibition of gladiators was not made up from the class of men which managers are in the habit of pitting against each other; that is, slaves sold on the platform and free men who are ready to sell their lives. In every case the service of the men who fought was voluntary and without compensation. For some were sent by their chieftains to display an example of the courage inbred in their tribe; some declared on their own motion that they would fight to please the1 general; in other cases rivalry and the desire to compete led them to challenge or, if challenged, not to refuse. Some who had been unable or unwilling to end their differences by a legal hearing, after agreeing that the disputed property should fall to the victor, settled the matter with the sword. Men also of no obscure family but conspicuous and distinguished, Corbis and Orsua, being cousins and competing for the post of chief of a city called Ibes, declared that they would contend with the sword. Corbis was the older in years. Orsua's father had lately been chief, having succeeded to an elder brother's rank upon his death. When Scipio desired to settle the question by a hearing and to calm their anger, they both said they had refused that request to their common relatives, and that they were to have as their judge no other god or man than Mars. The older man was confident in his strength, the younger in the bloom of his youth, each preferring death in the combat rather than to be subject to the rule of the other. Since they could not be made to give up such madness, they furnished the army a remarkable spectacle, demonstrating how great an evil among mortals is the ambition to rule. The older man by his skill with arms and by his cunning easily mastered the brute strength of the younger. In addition to this gladiatorial show there were funeral games so far as the resources of the province and camp equipment permitted. (Livy 28.21.1–10)

Scipio Aemilianus, perhaps inspired by this, sought even more novelty by holding Greek-style games after defeating the Macedonian King Perseus in 168 BC, favouring athletic over gladiatorial contexts. He may have felt that he had to show the Greeks, whom he had just conquered, that the Romans were not just a bunch of bloodthirsty barbarians (although, technically, that is exactly what they were in Greek eyes).

Back in Rome, as a result of an expensive animal hunt put on by Fulvius Nobilior in 186 BC (which we shall come to shortly), a general limit on the cost of games was introduced in the year 179. Nevertheless, the gladiatorial escalation continued apace. It seems 174 BC was a bad year if you were a gladiator:

> Many gladiatorial games were given that year, some of them unimportant; one was noteworthy beyond the rest, that of Titus Flamininus, which he gave to commemorate the death of his father, lasted four days, and was accompanied by a public distribution of meats, a banquet and scenic performances. The climax of a show which was big for that time was that in three days seventy-four gladiators fought. (Livy 41.28.9–11)

Gladiatorial combat was not an exclusively Roman taste. After Aemilianus' Greek games, the Syrian King Antiochus IV decided to indulge in some one-upmanship and he staged gladiatorial games at Daphne, near Antioch (Syria). These games began with a magnificent parade of armed men, including 250 pairs of gladiators, and lasted 30 days in total. In his defence, Antiochus had spent time in Rome as a hostage, so may have developed a taste for gladiatorial games then. Alternatively, he may have had a well-honed sense of how to needle Scipio in exactly the right way.

The expense of games inevitably spiralled upwards along with their duration and the number of performers, but cost was not the only thing increasing. Since gladiatorial combat was usually fought in the form of single matched pairs, large numbers of gladiators took a proportionally longer time to process: 250 pairs, assuming they took an average of 10 minutes each to fight to a result, would represent more than 40 hours of combat.

In 160 BC, when the great general Lucius Aemilius Paullus Macedonicus died, it was to be the occasion for something truly spectacular. There was, however, a problem: two of Macedonicus' four sons had been given up for adoption (a common ploy amongst the not-so-well-to-do aristocracy) and Fabius, the remaining natural son, could not afford the games. One of the adopted brothers (Scipio Aemilianus, who became the adoptive son of Scipio Africanus) came to the rescue:

> Scipio, knowing that his brother was by no means well off, gave up the whole inheritance, which was estimated at more than sixty talents, to him in order that Fabius might thus possess a fortune equal to his own. This became widely known, and he now gave an even more conspicuous proof of his generosity. His brother wished to give a gladiatorial show on the occasion of his father's funeral, but was unable to meet the expense, which was very considerable, and Scipio contributed the half of it out of his own fortune. The total expense of such a show amounts to not less than thirty talents if it is done on a generous scale. (Polybius 31.28.3–6)

Thirty talents was around 750,000 sesterces and nearly ten times what Nobilior paid for his *venatio*.

*Gallus ('Gaul')*
- Armour: helmet, mail
- Special feature: unknown
- Period: Republican
- Common opponent: unknown

The above list of events involving gladiators during the period of the middle Republic is unlikely to be comprehensive, not least because portions of Livy's text are missing and survive only as summaries, but also because historians do not seem to have been very interested in gladiatorial combat in its early days, although they may not have been in tune with the *zeitgeist*. The playwright Terence, writing in the middle of the 2nd century BC, observed wistfully that gladiatorial shows were now more popular than dramatic performances. He may have been slightly bitter that an audience ran out of one of his plays when they heard there were gladiators nearby.

## Animal entertainments

Animal entertainments, whether as staged hunts or as combat against exotic animals, seem to have had a completely different origin to gladiatorial combat. There is a connection with the various Hellenistic kingdoms around the Mediterranean which Rome encountered from the 3rd century BC onwards as it expanded its influence – not least because these were familiar with elephants and even used them in warfare. Indeed, it can be argued that the Roman fascination with exotic animals began with elephants. In 275 BC, Manius Curius Dentatus celebrated a triumph after his victory over the invader Pyrrhus, the king of Epirus (a real, rather than Pyrrhic, victory), which was that part of Greece nearest to the heel of Italy. Dentatus was the first to exhibit elephants in this triumph – four of them, according to Eutropius, who admittedly was writing about five centuries later. Such was their popularity that it will come as no surprise that Lucius Caecilius Metellus felt obliged to display 140 elephants a few years later, after defeating the Carthaginian commander Hasdrubal at the Battle of Panormus in 251 BC. However, there clearly came a point when just seeing exotic animals was not enough and the desire to see them killed took over. According to Pliny the Elder:

Verrius informs us that they fought in the Circus, and that they were slain with javelins, for want of some better method of disposing of them; as the people neither liked to keep them nor yet to give them to the kings. Lucius Piso tells us only that they were brought into the Circus; and for the purpose of increasing the feeling of contempt towards them, they were driven all round the area of that place by workmen, who had nothing but spears blunted at the point. The authors who are of opinion that they were not killed, do not, however, inform us how they were afterwards disposed of. (Pliny, *Natural History* 8.6.4)

In 167 BC, in a fit of inventive genius, Aemilius Paullus used elephants to crush deserters in a novel form of public execution. This was repeated by his son, Scipio Aemilianus, in 146 BC during his triumphal games after the successful defeat and destruction of Carthage (now part of Tunis in Tunisia) in the Third Punic War.

The fact that some of the Hellenistic kingdoms also maintained animal parks for hunting purposes may well have influenced the Romans. These had obviously become a way of demonstrating the wide range of their trading links (and thereby status), as well as providing some exotic hunting for idle kings. In 275/4 BC, the king of Egypt, Ptolemy II Philadelphus, staged a day-long procession of exotic animals in honour of the god Dionysus through the streets of Alexandria. This was led by 24 chariots drawn by elephants, followed by lions, leopards, panthers, camels, antelopes, wild asses and ostriches – apparently in pairs – plus a bear, a giraffe and a rhinoceros for good measure. The fact that this occurred on the streets of the city demonstrates that it was fairly and squarely aimed at pleasing the public as much as the god. It united showing off the breadth of one's domain by illustrating its wildlife diversity with the function of pleasing the masses; the added Roman value was almost inevitably going to be massacring all these animals brought to the capital at great expense. It was conspicuous consumption on a phenomenal and very bloody scale.

After the elephantine delights provided by Dentatus and his imitators, exotic animal displays in Rome became more ambitious. The comic playwright Plautus, writing at the end of the 3rd century BC, mentions 'ocean sparrows' in the circus, meaning ostriches (the Romans were already normalising these exotic African imports with nicknames). In 186 BC, Marcus Fulvius Nobilior staged the first recorded *venatio* or wild animal hunt with lions and panthers, to mark his military accomplishments in Greece, although his expenditure (spending money he had raised in Spain) was capped at 80,000 sesterces by the Senate. The animals probably came from Africa, since the Senate moved rapidly to restrict animal imports from there, probably as a result of this. This begs the question of where Nobilior got the idea for his event. Some have suggested that it developed from a Greek tradition (thanks to a comment by Theodoric in the 6th century AD), whilst others have pointed towards evidence for hunting in Etruscan tomb paintings. There may even have been some connection with the *Ludi Florales*, a religious festival where hares and deer were hunted in the Circus Maximus.

In 169 BC, there was an animal spectacle held in the Circus Maximus, organised by the aediles Scipio Nasica and Lentulus where they exhibited 63 *Africani* (the word could mean leopards or panthers) and 40 bears and elephants. (Aediles were city

*Samnis ('Samnite')*
- Armour: helmet, armguard, greave, curved rectangular shield
- Special feature: short sword
- Period: Republican

magistrates who held office for one year and were responsible for the upkeep of public buildings and the provision of public festivals, which came to include putting on the games.) The limit on spending that the Senate imposed in 179 BC following Nobilior's *venatio* was finally overturned in 114 BC by Gaius Aufidius – a tribune who was looking after the interests of the people (who wanted more spectacle, not a spending cap).

By the end of the 2nd century BC, it was becoming increasingly clear that the forum was not the optimum space for holding games. The shape and proportions were wrong (it was rectangular and for some spectators it was too long to see what was happening at the other end) and there were obstructions such as statues and other monuments blocking the view. One solution was to erect temporary seating to provide some elevation and, naturally, charge for it. This did not go down well with the poor and Gaius Gracchus, a particularly proactive (or, to others, meddlesome) tribune of the people decided to act:

> The people were going to enjoy an exhibition of gladiators in the forum, and most of the magistrates had constructed seats for the show round about, and were offering them for hire. Caius ordered them to take down these seats, in order that the poor might be able to enjoy the spectacle from those places without paying hire. But since no one paid any attention to his command, he waited till the night before the spectacle, and then, taking all the workmen whom he had under his orders in public contracts, he pulled down the seats, and when day came he had the place all clear for the people. (Plutarch, *Gaius Gracchus* 12.3-4)

## Formalisation

By the time of the Second Punic War, at the end of the 3rd century BC, it is probable that there were already gladiatorial schools and a formalised system for training gladiators, although these were obviously privately run. The general Cornelius Scipio, later to be known as Africanus for his eventual victory over Hannibal in North Africa, focused on Roman army training with some form of arms drill, but it was not yet the gladiatorial system. It would take another century before it was realised that the gladiatorial system could bring something to Roman army training that had, until then, been lacking. The results would speak for themselves. In fact, once it was introduced, the close relationship between gladiatorial and military training was to remain in place for at least four centuries, until such time as the army's weaponry began to evolve away from the traditional gladiatorial *armaturae*.

At the same time, the state insinuated its way into the business of organising games, which was threatening to become the preserve of rich and powerful men. The aediles, magistrates (first two, and later four of them) responsible for public buildings and the organising of festivals and, ultimately *munera* or games, were apparently directly involved in procuring animals for the games, as evidenced by Scipio Nasica and Lentulus in 169. Institutional control of the games was increasing, but there was still room for private enterprise.

# CHAPTER 3

# RISE OF THE GLADIATORS

*Plays, farces, spectacles, gladiators, strange beasts, medals,
pictures, and other such opiates, these were for ancient
peoples the bait toward slavery, the price of their liberty,
the instruments of tyranny.*

Étienne de La Boétie, *Discourse on Voluntary Servitude*

## Popularity and politics

REPUBLICAN ROME ENTERED AN EXTREMELY DANGEROUS phase in
the last century BC, as already powerful men became ever more
powerful and politics became about the competition between
great men. For such men, any means of bolstering their power
and influencing the mob became invaluable and gladiatorial
games became just one weapon in this armoury. The Roman
aristocracy were by now well aware of the efficacy of these shows
and they lost no opportunity to exploit them.

A major change came in 105 BC when a gladiatorial
performance was first held in a theatre in Rome under the
consuls Rutilius and Manlius (Rutilius will reappear later in
another context, but still with a gladiatorial connection). This
was the beginning of more permanent, less ad hoc venues, for

gladiatorial shows, and a palpable sign of the change of emphasis between funerary ritual and entertainment. They put on the display in their official capacity as magistrates, ostensibly to encourage the Roman populace to maintain a warlike spirit during a time of peace.

Marius, the great reformer of the Roman army at the end of the 2nd and beginning of the 1st century BC found a rather unusual aid in predicting the outcome of gladiatorial contests:

> Then she got audience of the women and gave them proofs of her skill, and particularly the wife of Marius, at whose feet she sat when some gladiators were fighting and successfully foretold which one was going to be victorious. In consequence of this she was sent to Marius by his wife, and was admired by him. (Plutarch, *Life of Marius* 17.2)

What does not seem to have been considered is that this Syrian woman may just have had a very good eye for 'form' amongst gladiators, rather than the power of prophecy, and that luck may also have played its part.

The import of exotic animals to be killed for the crowds also continued. When Quintus Scaevola was curule aedile in 104 BC, he brought in the first lions to Rome, according to Pliny the Elder; then Lucius Cornelius Sulla, whilst praetor in

*Andabata*
- Armour: mail, helmet
- Special feature: blindfolded
- Period: Republican
- Common opponent: *andabata*

93, produced 100 maned lions, only to be outdone by Gnaeus Pompeius – better known nowadays as Pompey – with 600 lions, 315 of them with manes, and so on. Lion escalation became the *munera* in a roaring microcosm.

The fascination with gladiators had its darker aspects too. Republican Roman society was heavily dependent upon slave labour, especially on the *latifundia*, the great agricultural estates that had been created by wealthy landowners buying up the original yeoman farmers' lands. The whole business of gladiatorial combat was founded in the misery of slavery and the slender hope that being really good at it ultimately offered a way out. Equally, the threat posed by communities of skilled killers at the heart of civil society did not escape the ordinary citizen and their fears were to be realised in the 1st century BC with one of their worst nightmares: a slave revolt led by gladiators who thought they had found another way out.

## Spartacus

Subject of a play, several historical novels, a ballet, a blockbuster film starring Kirk Douglas, a successful television series and several rock albums; who has not heard of Spartacus? A freedom fighter, socialist hero and enemy of Rome, he has become many things to many people, but the reality of the uprising led by him exposed weaknesses and fears in the Roman Republic which were to have long-term consequences.

As a background, it is worth pointing out that Sulla, the first of the new generation of warlords and dictator between 81 and 79 BC, had captured Thracians during his campaign against Mithridates, the king of Pontus, during the 80s BC. This is one possible origin for the *thraex* type of gladiator, although the Romans certainly knew of the Thracians before this and were to encounter them again. It should also be pointed out that Spartacus is said to come from Thrace in our sources, not that he fought as a Thracian gladiator (*thraex*).

The sources for the war with Spartacus are painfully scarce and most of what we know about him was written about two centuries after his revolt.

A certain Lentulus Batiatus had a school of gladiators at Capua, most of whom were Gauls and Thracians. Through no misconduct of theirs, but owing to the injustice of their owner, they were kept in close confinement and reserved for gladiatorial combats. Two hundred of these planned to make their escape, and when information was laid against them, those who got wind of it and succeeded in getting away, seventy-eight in number, seized cleavers and spits from some kitchen and sallied out. On the road they fell in with wagons conveying gladiators' weapons to another city; these they plundered and armed themselves. Then they took up a strong position and elected three leaders. The first of these was Spartacus, a Thracian of Nomadic stock, possessed not only of great courage and strength, but also in sagacity and culture superior to his fortune, and more Hellenic than Thracian. (Plutarch, *Crassus* 8.1–2)

There are a number of interesting details embedded in this account. First, the gladiators in Batiatus' training school do not appear to have had access to any weapons on the site and were forced to improvise using kitchen implements. This may be because the armoury was in an adjacent but not accessible

*Bestiarius ('beast-fighter')*
- Armour: none
- Special feature: shafted weapon
- Period: Republican and Imperial
- Common opponent: *wild animals*

*Provocator ('challenger')*
- Armour: helmet breastplate, armguard, greave, curved rectangular shield
- Special feature: short sword
- Period: Republican and Imperial
- Common opponent: *eques; provocator; murmillo*

location; indeed, at Pompeii, the only weapons found along with all the armour were daggers. Second, gladiators weapons intended for use in *munera* were moved around in convoys, presumably separately from the gladiators themselves. Finally, there seems to be an implication that it was not normal to keep gladiators in 'close confinement'.

Spartacus' small force immediately began to attract support from the many slaves who worked the land and ran those vast estates of southern central Italy. The Romans had dealt with slave uprisings before, but never one with such military expertise at its head. This immediately highlighted the ambivalent nature of the relationship between gladiators and soldiers: because their styles of hand-to-hand combat were so similar.

If their tactics were sound, inspired even, then so too was their strategy, at first. Taking refuge on Mount Vesuvius, overlooking the Bay of Naples, they repeatedly defeated over-confident Roman armies sent against them until, betrayed by the Cilician pirates who were supposed to provide passage out of Italy, they were finally crushed by M. Licinius Crassus, the richest man in Rome and one of the top warlords.

Intriguingly, a monochromatic fresco from Pompeii, thought to date to between 100 and 70 BC, has been suggested as

*Spartaks graffito from Pompeii (drawing by M. C. Bishop)*

depicting Spartacus himself. It shows two combatants on foot
with large rectangular shields, two mounted armed men with
oval or circular shields and a trumpeter, all labelled in Oscan
(the local language before Latin supplanted it). One mounted
figure, named SPARTAKS in reverse (Oscan was written right
to left), is being speared in the thigh by a pursuing rider. Some
scholars believe this shows Spartacus depicted in his final battle
(the historian Appian mentioned that he was wounded in the
thigh by a spear, although no mention is made of him being
mounted). Others suggest that it may in fact show a gladiatorial
contest pre-dating the Spartacus War, pointing to the trumpeter
and what might be an altar. There is no easy solution to this
conundrum, other than to note the coincidence of the name
(Spartaks/Spartacus), location (Pompeii, within sight of
Vesuvius) and the date (100–70 BC).

The Romans had long memories and Spartacus provided them
with an additional fear to set beside their traditional dislike of
northern barbarians (which dated back to the sack of Rome by
Gauls in 390 BC): distrust of gladiator armies. In the future,
only the direst of military situations would see Rome's leaders
resorting to recruiting forces composed of gladiators.

Spartacus is perhaps more important for his effect on the
modern period (and in particular the present-day impression
of gladiators) than for his impact upon Rome. The surviving
historical records are sparse for a very good reason: he was not
thought to have been particularly important. Although at the
time he posed a very real threat to the Roman state, it was never
insuperable and he was certainly no Hannibal. In the end, skill

in the arena did not transfer to the real world on a long-term basis, but it can at least be said that he is the only gladiator ever to have inspired a ballet and its accompanying suite of music.

## The warlords and civil war

With Spartacus out of the way, the Republic could resume its old course. The aristocracy had realised that the popularity of these games also made them a valuable political tool for securing votes and any excuse was found to hold them. The association between funerary games and gladiatorial combat may have been growing ever more tenuous, but it did not completely disappear, as an inscription from Carinola in Campania dating to around 60 BC (and maintaining the association with food noted above) attests:

> Lucius Papius Polio of the Teretine tribe, son of Lucius, member of the Board of Two, gave a feast of spiced honey wine and cakes in honour of his father Lucius Papius of the Falernian tribe, son of Lucius, for all the colonists of Sinuessa and Caedex, and a show of gladiators and a dinner for the colonists at Sinuessa and to the Papii. He set up a memorial at a cost of 12,000 sesterces from the will and with the approval of Lucius Novercinius Pollio, son of Lucius, of the Pupinian tribe. (*CIL* I, 1578)

*Eques* ('horseman')
- Armour: helmet
- Special feature: mounted, wearing tunic
- Period: Republican and Imperial
- Common opponent: *eques; provocator*

The last century of the Roman Republic saw the rise of great men like Crassus, Pompey the Great and most prominently Julius Caesar, who commanded armies loyal to them, rather than to the state, and gladiatorial games became just another means for them to assert political influence. They have to be seen in the context of the triumph, an honour awarded to a victorious general (although preferably not having defeated another Roman) at the close of campaigning. The triumph was a spectacle in its own right and had its similarities with the games, affording the general (who was also a politician, of course) a chance to show off his accomplishments and, inevitably, wealth. In 81 BC, at the tender age of just 24, Pompey even tried to use elephants to pull his triumphal chariot as he rode along the traditional route through the centre of Rome, only to find they would not fit through one of the arches he had to pass through, so the more usual horses were reluctantly substituted.

In 66 BC, Lucius Licinius Murena wished to sponsor particularly spectacular games, whilst he was praetor, for direct political aims and Cicero was quite open in describing his intentions a few years later when defending him from a charge of bribery:

> But if we ourselves, who, from our constant business, have but little time for amusement, and who are able to derive many pleasures of another sort from our business itself, are still pleased and interested

*Hoplomachus ('heavily armed fighter')*
- Armour: helmet, chest plate, greave(s)
- Special feature: spear
- Period: Republican and Imperial
- Common opponent: *thraex; murmillo*

by exhibitions of games, why should you marvel at the ignorant multitude being so? (Cicero, *Pro Murena* 39)

In other words, if the 'ignorant multitude' could be swayed by the provision of such games, then they were fair game. By 65 BC, Julius Caesar hoped to provide a staggering 320 pairs of gladiators at the games during his aedileship, ostensibly to mark the death of his father (an event that had taken place 20 years earlier). Clearly this was a blatant ploy to curry favour with the ordinary people from whom he drew his political support. Alarmed, the senate moved to limit the number or pairs he could show, partly because that many armed men in the city could be seen as a serious threat to the status quo. Once again, the fear of gladiators went hand-in-hand with the love of watching gladiatorial combat. Worse was to come.

In 63 BC, the nobleman L. Sergius Catilina attempted to lead a coup (usually known as the Catilinarian Conspiracy) against the existing government. The 'army' he had assembled was largely composed of assorted thugs and disaffected citizens, but the establishment saw the danger and reacted, moving all gladiators within Rome to Capua.

The gladiators which he thought would be his most numerous and most trusty band, although they are better disposed than part of the patricians, will be held in check by our power. (Cicero, *Against Catiline* 2.26)

As a result of Catilina's actions, the Senate subsequently passed a resolution that most gladiators had to be based outside of Rome to avoid a repetition of these events.

Pompey the Great found that providing spectacles could have its downside. In 55 BC, he had arranged for some elephants to fight against Gaetulian warriors from North Africa in the Circus Maximus. Unfortunately, things did not go to plan:

In the second consulship of Pompeius, at the dedication of the temple of Venus Victrix, twenty elephants, or, as some say,

*Thra(e)x ('Thracian')*
- Armour: helmet, greaves, armguard, small circular or square shield (*parma*)
- Special feature: angled sword (*sica*)
- Period: Republican to Imperial
- Common opponent: *murmillo*

seventeen, fought in the Circus against a number of Gaetulians, who attacked them with javelins. One of these animals fought in a most astonishing manner; being pierced through the feet, it dragged itself on its knees towards the troop, and seizing their bucklers, tossed them aloft into the air: and as they came to the ground they greatly amused the spectators, for they whirled round and round in the air, just as if they had been thrown up with a certain degree of skill, and not by the frantic fury of a wild beast. (Pliny, *Natural History* 8.7)

Cicero (who was busy defending a friend in the courts, so not an eyewitness) noted the result:

The last day was that of the elephants, on which there was a great deal of astonishment on the part of the vulgar crowd, but no pleasure whatever. Nay, there was even a certain feeling of compassion aroused by it, and a kind of belief created that that animal has something in common with mankind. (Cicero, *Letters to his Friends* 7.1)

The audience seemed to be siding with the elephants, which was not part of the plan. Then there was another rather alarming development, particularly for the stadium staff:

The elephants attempted, too, by their united efforts, to break down the enclosure, not without great confusion among the people who surrounded the iron gratings. (Pliny, *Natural History* 8.7)

By this point, Pompey may justifiably have concluded that he was extremely unlucky when it came to using elephants in public displays.

Gladiators were not only performers in the arena. They began to appear as strong-arm men to support political rivals. When the admittedly rather irritating Cato (famed for his old-fashioned Republican values) opposed a move to allow Pompey to enter Rome with armed men (traditionally not allowed), attempts were made to intimidate Cato and his allies:

When Cato paused in the forum and saw the temple of Castor and Pollux surrounded by armed men and its steps guarded by gladiators, and Metellus himself sitting at the top with Caesar, he turned to his friends and said: 'What a bold man, and what a coward, to levy such an army against a single unarmed and defenceless person!' (Plutarch, *Life of Cato* 27.4)

Caesar's founding of his new gladiatorial training school for 5,000 gladiators, the *Ludus Iuliani* at Capua, was viewed with suspicion not just because it threatened a stranglehold on the

*Veles ('lightly armed')*
- Armour: small round shield
- Special feature: spear
- Period: Republican to Imperial
- Common opponent: unknown

supply of gladiators to *munera*, but also because it could provide loyal gladiatorial thugs whenever he needed them to make a political point.

In 52 BC, Caius Scribonius Curio introduced a novel development: a double theatre that could be rotated to form an amphitheatre. Caesar made some improvements to the forum, adding subterranean tunnels and trapdoors through which scenery and animals could be introduced. In doing so, he anticipated the features of later amphitheatres, but Dio suggests he also imitated Curio in building an amphitheatre, albeit non-rotating:

> He built a kind of hunting-theatre of wood, which was called an amphitheatre from the fact that it had seats all around without any stage. In honour of this and of his daughter he exhibited combats of wild beasts and gladiators. (Dio 43.22.3)

These were temporary timber structures that attempted to maximise the available space. It was Caesar who also introduced a new form of entertainment: sham naval battles (*naumachia*), as part of the entertainments accompanying his quadruple triumph in 46 BC (which, as noted above, doubled as a commemoration of his daughter Julia, thereby maintaining a funerary link). Now whether these *naumachia* can be counted as true gladiatorial

*Venator ('hunter')*
- Armour: none
- Special feature: spear
- Period: Republican to Imperial
- Common opponent: *wild animals*

contests (did the participants have training schools? did they practice regularly?) is a moot point, but they eventually became part of the *munera* as one of the *spectacula* on offer.

Caesar had a special waterproofed basin constructed on a marshy part of the Campus Martius for a battle to be fought between the Carthaginian and Egyptian fleets. There were allegedly 4,000 oarsmen and 1,000 marines (all prisoners of war) in two-, three- and four-banked galleys and the event attracted so many visitors that people were camping on the streets. Naval warfare at the time tended to consist of ships ramming each other and then the crews effectively fighting a land battle at sea. The whole thing would have been scaled down (a real sea-going galley might have several hundred rowers on it) but would nevertheless have provided an exciting spectacle. Caesar later filled in the lake and also planned to build a temple to Mars on it, although this was never actually constructed. He had definitely started something, however.

Gladiatorial combat and its derivatives – animal hunting and naval battles – had become a political tool, an increasingly lavish entertainment (despite occasional checks and balances) and even an architectural driving force. Nevertheless, the taste for gladiatorial combat continued unabated. Indeed, on the day that Julius Caesar was assassinated in 44 BC, it was apparently no accident that gladiators were performing nearby in the Theatre of Pompey.

The death of Caesar marked the beginning of the end for the Republic and the arrival of a new phase for Rome. In violent times, the demand for gladiators showed no signs of decreasing just yet.

# CHAPTER 4

---

# AT THE PEAK

*At any rate, gladiators never charged with a crime are
offered in sale for the games so that they may become
the victim of public pleasure.*

Tertullian, *Spectacles* 19

## The Julio-Claudians

THE END OF THE REPUBLIC AND beginning of the Empire in
the last few decades of the 1st century BC saw many changes,
not least in the field of gladiatorial games. The association with
celebrating the death of significant individuals with the deaths
of others evaporated and the by-product – the intense interest of
the crowd – became the dominant element. This was the origin
of the term *munus* (literally, a gift) for gladiatorial games: it was a
gift or bribe to the electorate. The beginnings of this process can
perhaps be seen with the construction of the stone amphitheatre
at Pompeii in 70 BC: a permanent venue for funerary games is a
slightly odd concept. Under Augustus (27 BC to AD 14), it was
quickly realised that the popular desire for entertainment could
be used to the advantage of the new regime. This was nicely

summed up towards the end of the 1st century AD by the poet Juvenal with his phrase *panem et circenses* ('bread and circuses'): provide the mob with free food and free shows and they could be controlled. However, it has also been suggested that Augustus saw a new direction in which games could be taken, by associating them with religious festivals, such as his *Quinquatrus* in 12 BC in honour of Minerva.

To underline the continued importance of the games, one of the first things that happened after the defeat of Antony and Cleopatra was the construction of Rome's first stone amphitheatre in 29 BC. Located on the Campus Martius, it was erected by the nobleman Statilius Taurus, who had commanded Octavian's land forces during the Battle of Actium.

Once he had established himself as the de facto emperor of what had formerly been the Roman Republic, Octavian (now known as Augustus) made sure that all of the prime political tools available to great men were under his control. He had inherited the *Ludus Iuliani* at Capua from his adoptive father and this was to provide the core of the new Imperial gladiatorial training school. Gladiators trained there were known as *Iuliani* until the time of Nero, when (because the school was renamed to honour him) they became *Neroniani*.

In 2 BC, following the example of his adoptive father, Caesar, Augustus arranged for a *naumachia*, which he himself described in the document known as the *Res Gestae* (roughly 'Achievements') of which more than one copy survives as an inscription. Since the original lake had been filled in, a new one had to be provided:

> I gave the people a spectacle of a naval battle, in the place across the Tiber where the grove of the Caesars is now, with the ground excavated in length 1,800 feet [532 m], in width 1,200 [355 m], in which thirty ships with rams, biremes or triremes, but many smaller, fought among themselves; in these ships about 3,000 men fought in addition to the rowers. (Augustus, *Res Gestae* 23)

The location he chose for his *naumachia* was thus on the other side of the Tiber, in the area now known as Trastevere. Other sources tell us that it was a re-staging of the Battle of Salamis (480 BC), between the Athenians and Persians. We know that an aqueduct was built specially to supply the water necessary (the Aqua Alsietina) and that there was an island in the middle linked to the shore with a bridge. It only seems to have been used once and was partly filled in even during Augustus' lifetime.

Augustus also flooded the Circus Flaminius in order to stage a crocodile hunt. He nevertheless made sure that the more traditional aspects of the games were attended to. In keeping with tradition, his were bigger and better, and he was not averse to boasting about it:

> Three times I gave shows of gladiators under my name and five times under the name of my sons and grandsons; in these shows about 10,000 men fought. Twice I furnished under my name spectacles of athletes gathered from everywhere, and three times under my grandson's name. I celebrated games under my name four times, and furthermore in the place of other magistrates twenty-three times. As master of the college I celebrated the Secular Games for the college of the Fifteen, with my colleague Marcus Agrippa, when Gaius Furnius and Gaius Silanus were consuls [17 BC]. Consul for the thirteenth time [2 BC], I celebrated the first games of Mars, which after that time thereafter in following years, by a senate decree and a law, the consuls were to celebrate. Twenty-six times, under my name or that of my sons and grandsons, I gave the people hunts of African beasts in the circus, in the open, or in the amphitheatre; in them about 3,500 beasts were killed. (Augustus, *Res Gestae* 22)

This was death as entertainment on a massive scale, even if allowance is made for some political licence in those numbers (in those eight gladiatorial shows with 10,000 combatants, were they *all* gladiators, or was he including *noxii* put to death in the lunchtime hiatus?).

Gladiatorial contests were by no means just confined to the huge public spectacles of the arena. They could also be staged as private entertainments by the wealthy and powerful. Writing in the 1st century AD, Nicolaus of Damascus' account (preserved in Athenaeus' writings) is worth citing in more detail:

> The Romans staged spectacles of fighting gladiators not merely at their festivals and in their theatres, borrowing the custom from the Etruscans, but also at their banquets. At any rate, it often happened that some would invite their friends to dinner, not merely for other entertainment, but that they might witness two or three pairs of contestants in gladiatorial combat; on these occasions, when sated with dining and drink, they called in the gladiators. No sooner did one have his throat cut than the masters applauded with delight at this feat. And there have even been instances when a man has provided in his will that his most beautiful wives, acquired by purchase, should engage in duels; still another has directed that young boys, his favourites, should do the same. But the provision was in fact disregarded, for the people would not tolerate this outrage, but declared the will void. (Athenaeus, 4.153f–154a)

Tiberius (AD 14–37), who withdrew from Rome to Capri, was not particularly interested in gladiatorial contests or the games in their broadest sense, but that does not mean they ceased altogether under his rule. He held games to mark the death of Augustus in AD 14 (subsequently added to the calendar as the Augustalia festival) and more games followed the next year:

> A show of gladiators, given in the name of his brother Germanicus, was presided over by Drusus, who took an extravagant pleasure in the shedding of blood however vile — a trait so alarming to the populace that it was said to have been censured by his father. Tiberius' own absence from the exhibition was variously explained. Some ascribed it to his impatience of a crowd; others, to his native morosity and his dread of comparisons; for Augustus had been a good-humoured spectator. (Tacitus, *Annals* 1.76)

Nevertheless, Tiberius' lack of enthusiasm, as noted here by Tacitus, prompted one of the leading gladiators of the time, Triumphus, to respond to the hiatus with the rueful comment 'what a glorious time is passed'. In fact, gladiators were to play an unwelcome part in events in Gaul, for in AD 21, a revolt broke out there led by two Romanised locals, Florus and Sacrovir. Florus, who was based in Augustodunum (Autun in France), raised an impressive army:

> His followers amounted to forty thousand; one-fifth armed on the legionary model; the rest with boar-spears, hangers, and other implements of the hunting-field. To these he added a contingent of slaves, destined for the gladiatorial ring and encased in the continuous shell of iron usual in the country: the so-called *cruppelarii* – who, if too weighty to inflict wounds, are impregnably fortified against receiving them. (Tacitus, *Annals* 3.43)

Two legions and their accompanying auxiliaries marched against them from the Rhineland and they met just to the north of Augustodunum. The soldiers were at first frustrated by the heavily armoured *crupellarii* but soon found ways of dealing with them:

> The cavalry enveloped the flanks, and the infantry attacked the van. On the wings there was no delay; in front, the iron-clad men offered a brief impediment, as their plating was proof against javelin and sword. But the legionaries caught up their axes and picks and hacked at armour and flesh as if demolishing a wall: others overturned the inert masses with poles or forks, and left them lying like the dead without an effort to rise again. (Tacitus, *Annals* 3.46)

Back in Rome, the games were still a vital part of the political career of those seeking office, since the audience – or, at least the male citizens amongst them – were potential voters. Entrepreneurs stepped in to fund games themselves and tried to turn a profit out of it, cutting corners where they deemed it desirable. As so often happens with penny-pinching and profiteering, this was to lead to disaster. In AD 27, an amphitheatre collapsed; Tacitus records the events:

> A certain Atilius, of the freedman class, who had begun an amphitheatre at Fidena, in order to give a gladiatorial show, failed both to lay the foundation in solid ground and to secure the fastenings of the wooden structure above; the reason being that he had embarked on the enterprise, not from a superabundance of wealth nor to court the favours of his townsmen, but with an eye to sordid gain. The amateurs of such amusements, debarred from their pleasures under the reign of Tiberius, poured to the place, men and women, old and young, the stream swollen because the town lay near. This increased the gravity of the catastrophe, as the unwieldy fabric was packed when it collapsed, breaking inward or sagging outward, and precipitating and burying a vast crowd of human beings, intent on the spectacle or standing around. Those, indeed, whom the first moment of havoc had dashed to death, escaped torture, so far as was possible in such a fate: more to be pitied were those whose mutilated bodies life had not yet abandoned, who by day recognized their wives or their children by sight, and at night by their shrieks and moans. The news brought the absent to the scene — one lamenting a brother, one a kinsman, another his parents. Even those whose friends or relatives had left home for a different reason still felt the alarm, and, as it was not yet known whom the catastrophe had destroyed, the uncertainty gave wider range for fear.
>
> When the fallen materials came to be removed, the watchers rushed to their dead, embracing them, kissing them, not rarely quarrelling over them, in cases where the features had been obliterated but a parity of form or age had led to mistaken identification. Fifty thousand persons were maimed or crushed to death in the disaster; and for the future it was provided by a decree of the senate that no one with a fortune less than four hundred thousand sesterces should present a gladiatorial display, and that no amphitheatre was to be built except on ground of tried solidity. (Tacitus, *Annals* 62–3)

The Emperor Gaius (AD 37–41) was much more enthusiastic about the games. Gaius was more commonly known by the nickname his father's soldiers had given him when he was a small boy: Caligula or 'Little Boots', since they gave him a pair of small military boots. Wayward by even the most charitable interpretation, Caligula's reign is inevitably seen through the lens of Tacitus' and Suetonius' accounts (often, for a modern reading or TV-viewing public, via Robert Graves' *I Claudius*). It was not thought particularly eccentric that he himself trained as a Thracian gladiator, since many members of the nobility indulged in arms drill of some kind. In much the same way, it would not attract comment if a UK prime minister or US president might go jogging regularly, but it would be thought odd if they started competing in professional athletics.

Having spent the vast fortune Tiberius had left, some 2.7 billion sesterces, Caligula was forced to come up with a solution. His ingenious idea for raising more money was to hold a rather unusual auction:

> He would sell the survivors in the gladiatorial combats at an excessive valuation to the consuls, praetors, and others, not only to willing purchasers, but also to others who were compelled very much against their will to give such exhibitions at the Circensian games, and in particular he sold them to men specially chosen by lot to have charge of such contests (for he ordered that two praetors should be chosen by lot to have charge of the gladiatorial games, just as had formerly been the custom); and he himself would sit on the auctioneer's platform and keep raising the bids. Many also came from outside to put in rival bids, the more so as he allowed any who so wished to employ a greater number of gladiators than the law permitted and because he frequently visited them himself. So people bought them for large sums, some because they really wanted them, others with the idea of gratifying Gaius, and the majority, consisting of those who had a reputation for wealth, from a desire to take advantage of this excuse to spend some of their substance and thus by becoming poorer save their lives. (Cassius Dio 59.14.1–4)

Claudius (AD 41–54) chose to celebrate the anniversary of his accession by holding gladiatorial games (without an animal hunt) at a rather unusual location: the Praetorian Camp. Presumably this took place on the exercise ground immediately outside the fortress. These games of course was in response to, and perhaps thanks for, the role the Guard played in his accession, when they supposedly found him hiding behind a curtain in the Imperial palace and decided they would make him emperor on a whim. Such is the narrative that has come down to us, but the cynical might suspect that a Praetorian-backed coup lay behind the original assassination of Caligula and elevation of Claudius to the purple. If so, this was indeed an appropriate way to mark the event.

It was under Claudius that a particularly significant sham naval battle (*naumachia*) took place in AD 52 on the Fucine Lake, some 85 km east of Rome. Some of these were held in bespoke lakes, also called *naumachia*, whilst other, smaller-scale events could be staged by flooding an arena (Roman warships had a very shallow draft so such flooded sites did not need to be very deep). It was significant because this was the occasion when the combatants, presenting themselves to the emperor before the start, proclaimed 'Hail, Emperor, those who are about to die salute you!' (*ave, imperator, morituri te salutant*). Although it is often thought this was repeated by all gladiators before a

*Arbelas ('hide-scraper') or scissor ('cutter')*
- Armour: helmet, mail or scale
- Special feature: semi-circular blade on a gauntlet
- Period: Imperial
- Common opponent: *arbelas; retiarius*

contest, this is the only time the phrase was actually used, so far as is known. Moreover, these were condemned men, not true gladiators. Less often reported is Claudius' witty response, 'or not'. Unfortunately, the combatants interpreted that remark as a pardon and they then took some persuading to get on with it and take part in the fight.

As might be expected, Nero (AD 54–68) was very keen on all forms of entertainment and it was he who was credited with introducing women gladiators into the arena. He built a wooden amphitheatre on the Campus Martius to replace the less-than-ideal amphitheatre of Statilius Taurus, which had been used up until then. It was impressively big (the poet Calpurnius Siculus wrote a breathless, awe-struck account of it) and sumptuously appointed, with gems adorning the arena wall and gilded columns. Nero even had a man buying up as much amber as possible between the Baltic and the Danube, which was then used to adorn the nets protecting the crowd from wild animals, stretchers for the dead bodies, as well as some of the weapons. The top of the arena wall was equipped with ivory rollers to prevent wild animals gaining purchase if they tried to scale it. As was later the case with the Colosseum, there were trap doors that allowed scenery to be moved up from below ground.

In AD 57, Nero banned provincial governors from providing gladiatorial games and wild beast hunts within the provinces. This not only showed that some had been doing it and thereby attracted his attention as potential rivals, but also that he fully realised the importance of patronage of the games. That same year he held a rather spectacular *munus* (which included a sham naval battle) in his amphitheatre:

> At the gladiatorial show, which he gave in a wooden amphitheatre, erected in the district of the Campus Martius within the space of a single year, he had no one put to death, not even criminals. But he compelled four hundred senators and six hundred Roman knights, some of whom were well to do and of unblemished reputation, to fight in the arena. Even those who fought with the wild beasts and

performed the various services in the arena were of the same orders. He also exhibited a naval battle in salt water with sea monsters swimming about in it; besides pyrrhic dances by some Greek youths, handing each of them certificates of Roman citizenship at the close of his performance. (Suetonius, *Nero* 12.1)

Cassius Dio provides some extra detail which not only suggests he was seeking to emulate Augustus with his sea battle between the Persians and Athenians, but that some very sophisticated drainage had been provided:

He suddenly filled the place with sea water so that fishes and sea monsters swam about in it, and he exhibited a naval battle between men representing Persians and Athenians. After this he immediately drew off the water, dried the ground, and once more exhibited contests between land forces, who fought not only in single combat but also in large groups equally matched. (Cassius Dio 61.9.5)

To provide the entertainers for his new amphitheatre, Nero had his own gladiatorial training school at Capua, the Ludus Neronianus, formerly known as the Ludus Iulianus, which had been set up by Julius Caesar. By one of the many ironies of his reign, the new amphitheatre was burnt down in the fire of AD 64.

# The Flavians

During the civil wars that followed Nero's death in AD 68, Otho (AD 69) raised an force of 2,000 gladiators to supplement his army. It subsequently switched sides to Vitellius (AD 69), before ending up in the service of Vespasian (AD 69–79). Unlike many Romans, they clearly had a keen eye for a likely winner. Whilst the theory of using gladiators in the field was sound, once again it proved to be flawed in practice:

Against Otho's gladiators, too, who were supposed to have experience and courage in close fighting, Alfenus Varus led up the troops called Batavians. They are the best cavalry of the Germans, and come from an island made by the Rhine. A few of the gladiators withstood these, but most of them fled towards the river, where they encountered cohorts of the enemy in battle array, and in defending themselves against these, were cut off to a man. (Plutarch, *Otho* 12.4–5)

The inauguration of the Flavian Amphitheatre (or Colosseum) in AD 80 under Titus (AD 79–81) is said to have seen 100 days of games held in the new structure. These were funded by the spoils from Vespasian's and Titus' war in Judaea.

The modern visitor to the Colosseum can clearly see the substructures or basement beneath the arena. The sources make it clear that the arena could be flooded and drained to allow for naval battles, in much the same way as Nero's amphitheatre on the Campus Martius was. Many scholars find this implausible but it would indeed be unusual if so many sources were wrong about such a fundamental detail. Some suggest this means that the basement in the Flavian Amphitheatre was not constructed until later and it had a solid floor to the arena at the start, whilst others think the basement was an original feature. Titus' inauguration of the new amphitheatre evidently did include a sea battle but the sources are confused over whether it was in the Colosseum or at a separate location.

The main contribution of Domitian (AD 81–96), himself a follower of the *murmillones*, came in the form of regulation. It was he who put a stop to anybody other than emperors mounting games in Rome and, once done, it was never revoked. Not only did his measures provide an imperial monopoly on garnering the affections of the populace through lavish displays, it also allowed them to rein in its more exuberant (and expensive) excesses.

With all the magnificence of Imperial games being help in Rome, it is easy to forget that smaller towns with arenas carried on providing their own games for their inhabitants. An inscription

*Colosseum remains (photo by Danbu14)*

from Allifae (Italy) shows how a local magistrate provided 30 pairs of gladiators as well as a hunt featuring animals from Africa, during the latter part of the 1st century AD. This *duovir*, Lucius Fadius Pierus, then held another *munus* a few months later with the aid of a 13,000 sesterce grant from the town council, with another 21 pairs of gladiators and accompanying hunt. Naturally, the provincial *munera* best known to us are those at Pompeii, where we have so much information about the entertainment offered to its inhabitants and it is easy to see how these events would have been mirrored across the empire.

## Nerva, Trajan and Hadrian

The next emperor, Nerva (AD 96–98), was barely in office long enough to appoint his successor, Ulpius Traianus. Trajan (AD 98–117) was one of Rome's great warrior emperors. His campaigns in Dacia (roughly modern Romania) and Mesopotamia (the region of Syria and Iraq between the Euphrates and the Tigris) became legendary for his successes and they generated both wealth and captives in large numbers. This inevitably provided the pick of new recruits for the gladiatorial schools, notably the *Ludus Dacicus*. At the conclusion of the Dacian Wars, he funded games in AD 107 that lasted 123 days. During these games, according to the historian Cassius Dio, 10,000 gladiators fought and 11,000 animals were killed. There was almost certainly an element of exaggeration here, since it seems unlikely that there were that many gladiators in the entire empire, but if the figure included captives forced to fight each other and criminals publicly executed in the arena, as often happened at such events, the number seems more reasonable. Moreover, since gladiators tended to fight in pairs, it was physically impossible to mount 5,000 combats in 123 days and fit in the mass slaughter of assorted interesting animals. Whatever the numbers, an inscription from Rome preserves the names of three of the men who participated in this event:

> M. Antonius Exochus, a Thracian from Alexandria, fought as a *tiro* against Araxes the imperial slave, on the second day of the games for the triumph of the deified Trajan in Rome, dismissed standing. In Rome, on the ninth day of the same games, he fought Fimbria, a free man who had fought nine times; Fimbria was dismissed. In Rome, at the same games ... (*CIL* VI, 10194)

Two years later, in 109, he provided new games in honour of the inauguration of the Baths of Trajan, set on the hillside next to the Colosseum and overlying the reviled Golden House of Nero. These games provided 117 days of entertainment spread over five months, between June and the end of October. In that time, 8,000 gladiators and over 10,000 wild animals were supplied to please the audience. Trajan was one of the last to hold a *naumachia*, digging a new basin in what is now Vatican City, near Castel Sant'Angelo, as part of the 109 extravaganza, although it was less than one fifth of the size of Augustus' basin.

Another such round of games was held by Trajan in AD 113, this time with 2,000 gladiators in combat over a period of four months. In his *Panegyric*, written for Trajan, Pliny the Younger thought he detected a purpose behind all this ceremonial death, seeing the witnessing of 'glorious wounds and contempt of death' as a way of enthusing the Roman population for war. This looks like a justification after the fact, but the same notion is found again later.

Although the funerary origins of gladiatorial games had been superseded by entertainment and politics, it had not been completely forgotten, as Pliny attests when writing to his friend Maximus:

> You did perfectly right in promising a gladiatorial combat to our good friends the citizens of Verona, who have long loved, looked up to, and honoured you; while it was from that city too you received that amiable object of your most tender affection, your late excellent wife. And since you owed some monument or public representation to her memory, what other spectacle could you have exhibited more appropriate to the occasion? Besides, you were so unanimously pressed to do so that to have refused would have looked more like hardness than resolution. The readiness too with which you granted their petition, and the magnificent manner in which you performed it, is very much to your honour; for a greatness of soul is seen in these smaller instances, as well as in matters of higher moment. I wish the African panthers, which you had largely provided for this purpose, had arrived on the day appointed, but though they were delayed by the stormy weather, the obligation to you is equally the same, since it was not your fault that they were not exhibited. (Pliny, *Letters* 6.34)

Hadrian (AD 117–38), like Trajan, was a military man through and through and had commanded legions and even provincial armies before he became emperor. His biographer noted that he provided six successive days of gladiatorial combat at one point, as well as 1,000 animals in the arena on his birthday. It was also recorded that he knew how to use gladiatorial weapons and liked to attend gladiatorial shows, although these facts did not attract the same opprobrium that was later the case for Commodus, probably because (unlike the latter) he was not performing publicly.

## The Antonines

Seen by Gibbon as the pinnacle of sophistication for Roman civilisation, the Antonine Age witnessed no real diminution in the fondness for gladiators. Antoninus Pius (AD 138–61), however, established a maximum cost for expenditure when mounting gladiatorial games, although that said more about his keeping a careful eye on the spending than it did about his attitude to gladiatorial performances. He was by no means averse to mounting his own games:

> He held games at which he displayed elephants and the animals called corocottae [possibly hyenas] and tigers and rhinoceroses, even crocodiles and hippopotami, in short, all the animals of the whole earth; and he presented at a single performance as many as a hundred lions together with tigers. (*Historia Augusta, Life of Antoninus Pius* 10.9)

Marcus Aurelius (AD 161–80) was uninterested in gladiators, rather than actively disliking them, but his brother and co-ruler, Lucius Verus (AD 161–9), liked both chariot racing and gladiatorial combat. His coming of age at 15 was marked in AD 145 by his adoptive father, the Emperor Antoninus Pius, putting on a games at which he sat between his brother and the emperor. Later, he was to entertain guests at his villa outside Rome with dinner-party gladiatorial matches, much as had been done in the good old days. His biographer, a rich source of nonsense and tittle-tattle, boasted that he even gave gladiators away to guests.

At one point during his Marcomannic Wars north of the Danube, Marcus Aurelius raised a band of gladiators to assist his campaign, naming them the *Obsequentes* ('The Compliant Ones'), a measure of how serious the situation had become.

In AD 177, concern over the size of the various forms of games led to the introduction of a law limiting the spending allowed: the *senatus consultum De Pretiis Gladiatorum Minuendiis*. There had apparently been attempts at some sort of limit under Augustus and Hadrian, but Marcus Aurelius implemented a complex system to make it work by ranking the relative costs of gladiators. Interestingly, they were not valued (and thus ranked) by type but rather by value, so a top level *retiarius* was worth the same as a top level *thraex* or *secutor* and so on. This enabled the overall cost of any *munus* to be worked out. This ranking of gladiators may in fact have been equated with the *palus* system within any gladiatorial school (*primus palus*, *secundus palus*, etc).

Marcus Aurelius' son, Commodus (AD 177–92), took his love of all things gladiatorial so far that he even liked to join in. His biographer said he 'lived with gladiators' and noted that

> He fought in the arena with foils, but sometimes, with his chamberlains acting as gladiators, with sharpened swords. (*Historia Augusta, Commodus* 5.5)

It was clearly slightly more than a hobby for him and verged on a dangerous obsession:

> He engaged in gladiatorial combats, and accepted the names usually given to gladiators with as much pleasure as if he had been granted triumphal decorations. He regularly took part in the spectacles, and as often as he did so, ordered the fact to be inscribed in the public records. It is said that he engaged in gladiatorial bouts seven hundred and thirty-five times.... It is related in records that he fought 365 gladiatorial combats in his father's reign. Afterwards, by vanquishing or slaying *retiarii*, he won enough gladiatorial crowns to bring the number up to a thousand. He also killed with his own hand thousands of wild beasts of all kinds, even elephants. And he frequently did these things before the eyes of the Roman people. (*Historia Augusta, Commodus* 11.10–12.12)

Again, as with Lucius Verus, much of this may have been fiction later attached to a deeply unpopular emperor, but there may still have been a core of truth behind it. What is significant are the details of gladiatorial tradition that such passages betray:

> At gladiatorial shows he would come to watch and stay to fight, covering his bare shoulders with a purple cloth. And it was his custom, moreover, to order the insertion in the city gazette of everything he did that was base or foul or cruel, or typical of a gladiator or a procurer – at least, the writings of Marius Maximus so testify. He entitled the Roman people the 'People of Commodus', since he had very often fought as a gladiator in their presence. And although the people regularly applauded him in his frequent combats as though he were a god, he became convinced that he was being laughed at, and gave orders that the Roman people should be slain in the Amphitheatre by the marines who spread the awnings. He gave an order, also, for the burning of the city, as though it were his private colony, and this order would have been executed had not Laetus, the prefect of the Guard, deterred him. Among other triumphal titles, he was also given the name 'Captain of the *Secutores*' six hundred and twenty times. (*HA, Commodus* 15.3–8)

On one occasion, Commodus took the opportunity to show off his skill as an archer:

> He shot arrows with crescent-shaped heads at Moroccan ostriches, birds that move with great speed, both because of their swiftness afoot and the sail-like nature of their wings. He cut off their heads at the very top of the neck; so, after their heads had been severed by the edge of the arrow, they continued to run around as if they had not been injured. (Herodian 1.15.5)

This may have been the same occasion when he issued a rather menacing threat to the watching senators (who included the historian Cassius Dio). Their response resembles that of many sane people to subsequent despots of questionable sanity:

Here is another thing that he did to us senators which gave us every reason to look for our death. Having killed an ostrich and cut off his head, he came up to where we were sitting, holding the head in his left hand and in his right hand raising aloft his bloody sword; and though he spoke not a word, yet he wagged his head with a grin, indicating that he would treat us in the same way. And many would indeed have perished by the sword on the spot, for laughing at him (for it was laughter rather than indignation that overcame us), if I had not chewed some laurel leaves, which I got from my garland, myself, and persuaded the others who were sitting near me to do the same ... (Cassius Dio 73.21.1–2)

Commodus decided to make a minor change or two to the enormous statue which gave its name to the Colosseum:

He removed the head of a huge Colossus which the Romans worship and which bears the likeness of the Sun, replacing it with his own head, and inscribed on the base not the usual imperial and family titles; instead of 'Germanicus' he wrote: 'Conqueror of a Thousand Gladiators'. (Herodian 1.15.9)

Suffice it to say that the last emperor who had put his own head on the Colossus had been Nero and that had not ended well. When Commodus' possessions were sold off after after his death by Helvius Pertinax (AD 193), they were found to include

*Crupellarius*
- Armour: plate, helmet
- Special feature: heavily protected
- Period: Imperial
- Common opponent: unknown

a gladiator's cloak and arms decorated with gold and jewels; also swords, such as those with which Hercules is represented, and the necklaces worn by gladiators (*HA, Pertinax* 8.3–4)

Commodus had a well-known fondness for being identified with Hercules and a bust of him in the guise of that hero is displayed in the Capitoline Museums in Rome.

## The Severans

Appropriately, Septimius Severus (AD 193–211) – whose first task was to deal with other pretenders to the purple – was proclaimed emperor in an amphitheatre (one of the two at Carnuntum in Austria) in AD 197. One of his opponents, Didius Julianus (AD 193 – who, his biographer sneered, had himself trained with gladiatorial weapons), attempted to arm the gladiators at Capua to form an army to oppose Severus, all to no avail.

The games continued unabated during Severus' reign, with him providing a show in Rome before he left for his Parthian Wars in the East. His son, Caracalla (AD 198–217) who murdered his brother Geta once their father was dead, was said to have liked the company of gladiators and charioteers (one of his nicknames was Tarautas, after an ugly gladiator of that name), but one tale about him provides an incidental detail of interest:

He took pleasure in seeing the blood of as many gladiators as possible; he forced one of them, Bato, to fight three men in succession on the same day, and then, when Bato was slain by the last one, he honoured him with a brilliant funeral. (Cassius Dio 78.6.2)

Clearly, it was not normal to expect a gladiator to fight three opponents in one day. Whilst on campaign in the East, based at Nicomedia, one of the ways he amused himself was to fight as a gladiator (although whether he competed in the arena or merely trained as one is unclear). Indeed, he celebrated his birthday there with games:

> Here it is said that when a defeated combatant begged him to spare his life, Antoninus said: 'Go and beg your opponent. I have no power to spare you.' And so the wretch, who would perhaps have been spared by his antagonist, had these words not been spoken, lost his life; for the victor did not dare to release him, for fear of appearing more humane than the emperor. (Cassius Dio 78.19.3)

## The crisis years

The old fear of gladiator armies resurfaced during the reign of Maximinus Thrax (AD 235–8), when a senatorial revolt threatened the Praetorian Guard in Rome:

> Gallicanus, by his reckless crime, brought civil war and widespread destruction upon the city. He persuaded the people to break into the public arsenals, where armour used in parades rather than in battle was stored, each man to protect himself as best he could. He then threw open the gladiatorial schools and led out the gladiators armed with their regular weapons; finally, he collected all the spears, swords, and axes from the houses and shops. The people, as if possessed, seized any tools they could find, made of suitable material, and fashioned weapons. They assembled and went out to the Praetorian Camp, where they attacked the gates and walls as if they were actually organizing a siege. The Praetorians, with their vast combat experience, protected themselves behind their shields and the battlements; wounding their attackers with arrows and long spears, they kept them from the walls and drove them back. With evening approaching, the besiegers decided to retire, since the civilians were exhausted and most of the gladiators were wounded. The people retreated in disorder, thinking that the few Praetorians would not dare to pursue so large a mob. But the Praetorians now threw open the gates and gave chase. They slaughtered the

gladiators, and the greater part of the mob also perished. (Herodian 7.11.6–9)

The notion that gladiatorial games hardened the population for war had been voiced by Pliny and reappears in the *Historia Augusta* (composed in the 4th century AD but using 2nd- and 3rd-century sources):

> Whence this custom arose, that emperors setting out to war gave an entertainment of gladiators and wild beasts, we must briefly discuss. Many say that among the ancients this was a solemn ritual performed against the enemy in order that the blood of citizens being thus offered in sacrifice under the guise of battle, Nemesis (that is a certain avenging power of Fortune) might be appeased. Others have related in books, and this I believe is nearer the truth, that when about to go to war the Romans felt it necessary to behold fighting and wounds and steel and naked men contending among themselves, so that in war they might not fear armed enemies or shudder at wounds and blood. (*Historia Augusta, Maximinus and Balbinus* 8.5–7)

Gordian I (AD 238) was not emperor for very long, but he was familiar with gladiatorial games. Before he was emperor and whilst he was aedile, he personally provided twelve *munera* (one a month for his term of office!) which included between 150 and 500 pairs of gladiators in each event. Once he had become emperor, he left his mark not only on the arena but also on the walls of the house of Pompey the Great (known as the *Domus Rostrata* from the fact the vestibule was decorated with the prows of captured pirate ships).

> There exists also today a remarkable wild-beast hunt of his, pictured in Gnaeus Pompey's *Domus Rostrata*; this palace belonged to him and to his father and grandfather before him until your privy-purse took it over in the time of Philip. In this picture at the present day are contained two hundred stags with antlers shaped like the palm of a hand, together with British stags, thirty wild horses, a hundred

wild sheep, ten elks, a hundred Cyprian bulls, three hundred red Moorish ostriches, thirty wild asses, a hundred and fifty wild boars, two hundred chamois, and two hundred fallow deer. And all these he handed over to the people to be killed on the day of the sixth exhibition that he gave. (*Historia Augusta, The Gordians*, 3.6–8)

Thus Gordian I's contribution to arena games was to introduce a level of interactivity for the audience which was previously unknown: they could actually participate in killing the wildlife assembled for their entertainment.

That same Philip (the Arab, AD 244–49) decided to hold the Secular Games in Rome in April of AD 248. These *Ludi Saeculares* marked the 1,000th anniversary of the traditional foundation of Rome in 753 BC. This had to be done in a significant way and, fortunately, there were a few spare beasts that could drawn upon.

There were thirty-two elephants at Rome in the time of Gordian (of which he himself had sent twelve and Alexander ten), ten elk, ten tigers, sixty tame lions, thirty tame leopards, ten belbi or hyenas, a thousand pairs of imperial gladiators, six hippopotami, one rhinoceros, ten wild lions, ten giraffes, twenty wild asses, forty wild horses, and various other animals of this nature without number. All of these Philip presented or slew at the Secular Games. All these animals, wild, tame, and savage, Gordian intended for a Persian triumph; but his official vow proved of no avail, for Philip presented all of them at the Secular Games, consisting of both gladiatorial spectacles and races in the Circus, that were celebrated on the thousandth anniversary of the founding of the City, when he and his son were consuls. (*Historia Augusta, The Gordians* 33.1–3)

The *Historia Augusta*'s biography of Probus (AD 276–82) has a particularly juicy tale to tell of the games he provided, whilst at the same time providing a cautionary tale over the use of such literary sources.

He also gave the Romans their pleasures, and noted ones, too, and he bestowed largesses also. He celebrated a triumph over the Germans and the Blemmyes, and caused companies from all nations, each of them containing up to fifty men, to be led before his triumphal procession. He gave in the Circus a most magnificent wild-beast hunt, at which all things were to be the spoils of the people. Now the manner of this spectacle was as follows: great trees, torn up with the roots by the soldiers, were set up on a platform of beams of wide extent, on which earth was then thrown, and in this way the whole Circus, planted to look like a forest, seemed, thanks to this new verdure, to be putting forth leaves. Then through all the entrances were brought in one thousand ostriches, one thousand stags and one thousand wild-boars, then deer, ibexes, wild sheep, and other grass-eating beasts, as many as could be reared or captured. The populace was then let in, and each man seized what he wished. Another day he brought out in the Amphitheatre at a single performance one hundred maned lions, which woke the thunder with their roaring. All of these were slaughtered as they came out of the doors of their dens, and being killed in this way they afforded no great spectacle. For there was none of that rush on the part of the beasts which takes place when they are let loose from cages. Besides, many, unwilling to charge, were despatched with arrows. Then he brought out one hundred leopards from Libya, then one hundred from Syria, then one hundred lionesses and at the same time three hundred bears; all of which beasts, it is clear, made a spectacle more vast than enjoyable. He presented, besides, three hundred pairs of gladiators, among whom fought many of the Blemmyes, who had been led in his triumph, besides many Germans and Sarmatians also and even some Isaurian brigands. (*Historia Augusta, Probus* 19, 1–8)

If this is an accurate account, there had been no letting up in the taste for or desire to provide lavish spectacles, despite the troubles of the Empire at this time. It does highlight one of the more unusual aspects of the whole 'bread and circuses' aspect of Roman society. Although there were snacks available to the audience, it had become a tradition to hand out free food in the form of gifts to the audience at *munera*. Often these were *missilia* (literally 'missiles') hurled into the audience in the form of small wooden balls bearing inscriptions which could be redeemed for those gifts, including food. Once the Colosseum came into use, its ticketing system provided a ready-made token scheme akin to lottery tickets. One of the things given away apparently included meat. Huge displays of wild animals, most of them inevitably slaughtered, meant the organisers were faced with a glut of meat which had to be disposed of, so it ended up being given away to the crowd.

Probus' games were evidently divided between the animal 'hunt' in the circus (probably the Circus Maximus) and the gladiatorial show in the arena (the Colosseum). That the games occurred seems highly likely, but one of the problems with our principal source, the *Historia Augusta*, is that historians harbour serious doubts over its accuracy when relating detail. Without independent verification, how is it possible to be sure that so much enticing material was not in fact fictional?

We do know that a rather alarming incident occurred during his reign, when 80 gladiators escaped after killing their keepers and set about plundering in Rome. Although Probus was able to deal with the incident, it must have struck a chord with all Romans and reminded them of Spartacus.

Amidst all the wearying excess, we find the first hints of a new attitude emerging from the Emperor Diocletian (AD 284–305):

### Diocletian and the tetrachy

Diocletian was the founder of the Roman tetrarchy (meaning rule-of-four). At the end of the troubled times of the 3rd century AD, the Roman empire was divided into two halves, the Eastern and the Western. Each of these had a senior emperor (or *Augustus*) and a junior emperor (or *Caesar*). Diocletian was *Augustus* of the Eastern Empire.

When Diocletian himself presented spectacles, after inviting all nations thereto, he was most sparing in his liberality, declaring that there should be more continence in games when a censor was looking on. (*Historia Augusta, Carus, Carinus, & Numerian* 20.3)

One of Diocletian's major reforms was his attempt to tackle the problem of inflation in the form of his *Edict on Maximum Prices* from AD 301. Included within this were limits for beasts imported for the games, that for a first-rate lion being 150,000 *denarii* (600,000 sesterces), whilst a second-rate one was listed at 125,000 *denarii* (500,000 sesterces). The same list rated a military saddle at 100 *denarii* (400 sesterces), for the sake of comparison, and it shows the huge prices these exotic animals could fetch. A mosaic from Piazza Armerina in Sicily (Italy), dated to the first half of the 4th century AD, illustrates such animals being rounded up and collected prior to shipping out. At least part of the reason for the high prices commanded by exotic wild animals may have been a direct result of the cumulative Roman demand for them impacting upon their populations, so that they became rarer in regions where they had once been common and had to be sourced from further afield.

Having followed the development of gladiatorial games from their inception right through to a point from which they start to decline, it is now appropriate to pause and examine the equipment they used, the places in which they fought, and what they could look forward to once they had been engaged to fight for their lives.

# CHAPTER 5

# HARDWARE AND VENUES

*Who does not reckon the contests of gladiators and wild*
*beasts among the things of greatest interest, especially*
*those which are given by you. But we, because we believe*
*that to watch a man be put to death is much the same*
*as killing him, avoid such spectacles.*

Athenagoras, *A Plea for the Christians* 35

WHEN WE THINK OF WHAT GLADIATORS looked like, two images inevitably dominate our mental picture. First there is the *Gladiator* movie (which is wrong in virtually every detail) and second there is the famous 1872 painting *Pollice Verso* by Jean-Léon Gérôme (which is extremely accurate). The former seems largely to have relied upon imagination, whereas the latter drew on mosaics, frescoes, graffiti and most especially actual finds of equipment from the excavations at Pompeii to depict gladiators in the arena.

Like Gérôme, our evidence for the dress and equipment of gladiators relies partly on representational evidence but also on archaeological finds. Sculpture could normally be much more detailed than mosaics (which can sometimes look like very low-resolution computer graphics), but mosaics and frescoes preserve colour (and most ancient sculpture, although originally coloured, has lost it over time). Thus a mosaic can use grey to

Pollice Verso *by Gérôme*

hint at steel, or orangey yellow for some form of copper alloy, providing us with more detail for our overall picture.

It is perhaps noteworthy that none of the known gladiator armour includes the sort of ownership inscriptions found on the equipment of Roman soldiers. The reason for this is simple: soldiers owned their equipment, whereas the arms and armour of gladiators belonged to their *ludus*.

## Dress, weapons and equipment

### *Dress*

The gladiator usually wore little except an elaborate loin cloth, the *subligaculum*. There are exceptions, such as the *equites*, who seem to have worn a full *tunica*, but the loin cloth was the normal garb for a whole range of types of gladiator. It was worn with a broad belt and appears to have been folded in a particular way in order to produce its distinctive, nappy-like appearance. One of the more common types was wrapped around the waist from behind, then the free end brought through the legs and folded back down on itself before being belted. The belt (*balteus*) itself seems to have been metallic and modelled on the belts of the Samnites (against whom the Romans had waged war during the 4th century BC).

## Swords

Gladiators got their name from their principal weapon, the sword or *gladius*. Although the short sword is often equated with the *gladius hispaniensis* – literally the 'Spanish sword' – which was introduced into the Roman army during the 2nd century BC, the Latin word *gladiator* occurs long before this and betrays the fact that the word *gladius* was just a generic term for a sword of any kind.

No certain gladiatorial swords as such survive, but there are many military swords to provide a comparison. The sword consisted of an iron blade with an integral tang to which a handle was fitted. The handle comprised three principal components: the hand guard, the hand grip and the pommel. The hand guard protected the user's hand on the grip, preventing another blade from sliding up. The grip provided purchase for the user, military examples often being hexagonal in cross-section and made out of cow long bones. The pommel acted as a counterweight to the blade but was also, like the hand guard, protection for the bearer's hand and could act as a handy weapon in its own right. The handle assembly was held onto the tang with a top nut, the tang being peened over it once it was attached, thereby providing a secure assembly. The pommel and top nut could then be used like the 'skull-crusher' on a Second World War commando dagger to deliver a very nasty blow at close quarters. Amongst gladiatorial weapons, the top nut also incorporated a ring to which the looped thong could be attached.

*Dimachaerus* ('two swords')
- Armour: none
- Special feature: shieldless, with two swords
- Period: Imperial
- Common opponent: *dimachaerus*

Scientific analysis of military swords shows how they were an ingenious combination of iron and steel, providing both the strength of steel at the edges of the blade, and softer, more flexible iron at the core of the blade. There are stories of the Spanish swords upon which Roman blades were modelled being capable of being placed on the head of a man, bending the tip and tang down to his shoulders, and then springing back to shape afterwards. Nevertheless, Roman swords were never designed for blade-on-blade fencing of the kind popular in movies, but rather for hand-to-hand combat – whether soldiers or gladiators – centring on combined use of the sword and shield.

There was some debate amongst the Romans over the best way to use the short sword – was it a cut or thrust weapon? In fact, it was ideally suited to either type of blow and sculpted reliefs show gladiators using them in both ways, unsurprisingly.

One of the characteristics of a gladiator's sword was that, unlike a soldier's sword, it was never used with a scabbard. The soldier needed to have his sidearm with him at all times, but used the scabbard to keep his hands free when he was not actually using the weapon. Gladiators were only armed when actually in the arena and so their swords had a looped thong attached to the pommel which the gladiator then wore around his wrist. If he

*Tiber relief with sword (photo by J. C. N. Coulston)*

dropped his sword for any reason, that loop meant he would not lose it completely and could easily recover the weapon. The loop is clearly visible on some of the surviving sculptural reliefs.

A number of swords were found at Pompeii but none of them came from the gladiatorial barracks nor had rings on top of their pommels, whilst the presence of scabbards confirms that they were not gladiatorial weapons. They probably belonged to the marines sent to assist the inhabitants of the Bay of Naples, since we know they were equipped just like soldiers.

The short sword actually went out of use with the army during the 2nd century AD and was replaced with the longer cavalry sword, the *spatha*. The short sword was reintroduced by cutting down broken longer swords in army units, but there is no evidence that the *gladius* ever fell from favour amongst gladiators.

Thracians used their own type of sword, the *sica* or sickle, a type of weapon derived from an agricultural implement and found in the eastern Danube basin. This originally had a curved blade with a single edge (on the inside of the curve), although gladiatorial weapons seem to have had an angle, rather than a

*Hippolytos the Thracian (photo by Carole Raddato)*

curve, in the blade. A wooden replica of a *sica* was found in a ditch at the Roman fort of Oberaden in Germany, possibly a *rudis* presented to a retired gladiator. Unlike the *gladius*, it was primarily designed as a cutting weapon.

## Daggers

Whatever their principal weapon might have been, every gladiator had a dagger. This was used to finish off an opponent once he had achieved his victory. It was also a vital back-up sidearm should a swordsman lose his primary weapon. The dagger is depicted in the reliefs from Lucus Feroniae where one sword fighter is stabbing his felled opponent in the neck, using a dagger in his left hand whilst still holding his sword in his right. It might also have been used by a gladiator trapped in the net of a *retiarius* to cut his way out, if he was lucky.

*Lucus Feroniae relief (photo by Sophie Hay)*

An example of such a dagger was found at Pompeii in the peristyle structure identified as the gladiatorial barracks. It had a one-piece bone handle, the grip being slightly swollen towards the middle so as to fit the hand, a hand guard shaped like the cross-bar of a T, and a small, ovoid pommel. The blade, although corroded, was around 30cm long and was rhomboidal in cross-section. Unlike military daggers, which generally had waisted blades, the Pompeii example had parallel edges. However, a typical military dagger from London was found with an atypical turned wooden handle fitted over its tang and it is possible that this too may have been used by a gladiator.

A four-spiked dagger (*quadrens*) is depicted on the tombstone of the *retiarius* Skirtos from Constanța (Romania). The use of this rather unusual weapon seems to be demonstrated by a femur bone from a gladiator cemetery in Ephesus.

# Shafted weapons

Some gladiators relied upon shafted weapons (also known as polearms). The *hoplomachus*, a gladiatorial interpretation of the Greek hoplite, was armed with a circular shield and a thrusting spear which gave him superior reach over a sword-armed opponent. The *retiarius* also used a shafted weapon – the trident (normally, but not exclusively, held in his right hand). The trident (*fuscina* or *tridens*) originated as a fisherman's weapon and it is shown being used both single- and double-handed. Not only do examples of the ferrous head survive (one from the harbour at Ephesus was 38.5cm long), but a skull from the gladiator cemetery there was found to have skull wounds exactly matching such examples, with the tines spaced 5cm apart. Animal fighters (*bestiarii*) and hunters (*venatores*) generally relied upon shafted weapons, although gladiators armed with swords and shields are occasionally shown fighting wild animals. Hunting spears, unlike the regular sort used by troops, often had sideways projections or lugs immediately below the head to prevent determined animals (especially wild boar) running up them to get at the weapon's owner.

Ancient spear shafts were not just cut from a length of timber but had to be grown specially as poles by coppicing suitable species of tree, such as ash or hazel. That way the shaft was much stronger, since the older, harder wood was at the core, whilst the younger, more supple material was nearer the surface. Indeed, hafting a weapon was every bit as important as heading it. Such considerations were extremely important for those who fought with the thrusting spear or trident as their principal weapon.

Mounted gladiators (*equites*) used spears as did some varieties of foot gladiator such as the *hoplomachus*. Against sword-armed opponents they provided an interesting match of reach over efficacy: the spear-armed gladiator had to keep his opponent at a distance, whilst the one armed with the sword had to get in close so that the spear was no longer effective. Spears and javelins

Bestiarius *spears an* Africanus *(photo by Carole Raddato)*

were normally held overarm in the classical world, although the *pilum*, the heavy javelin of the army, was held underarm for thrusting on occasion and the trident is shown being used in this way. Similarly, the hunting spear is sometimes depicted as being held two-handed against wild beasts.

## Helmets

Gladiators originally just used their native equipment and their helmets were open at the front and equipped with hinged cheek pieces at the sides, as was the case with Roman soldiers' helmets. Helmets like these can be seen on reliefs up to and including the time of Augustus (27 BC–AD 14). However, the 1st century AD saw gladiatorial helmets evolve quite considerably so that, by the time of the eruption of Vesuvius in AD 79, they were highly specialised pieces of headgear.

*Gladiator helmets from Pompeii (photo by M. C. Bishop)*

Examples from Pompeii included a broad brim, shaped and angled to deflect blows from the head, and thus fulfilling the purpose of both the neck guard and brow guard of a military helmet. The helmets also now enclosed the face of the wearer, only allowing him a limited view through hinged, meshed eye guards. This feature had the advantage of making it that bit harder to see one's opponent, thus increasing the drama of an encounter. Specific types of helmet were used by the various types of gladiators (with the exception of *retiarii* and *bestiarii*, who went bare-headed). The *murmillo* helmet had a broad brim and fore-and-aft crest like a fish fin, although whether this was the reason for their name or a reflection of it is unclear. The *secutor*, however, wore a helmet with no brim, small eyeholes and a low fore-and-aft crest. There was little by way of decoration in order to facilitate the deflection of the *retiarius'* trident. A bronze model of a *secutor* from Arles (France) has a hinged visor that lifts up to reveal the face of the gladiator, but it is unclear whether any real helmets mimicked this. *Thraex* helmets were distinguished from those of *murmillones* by a characteristic griffin head projecting from the front of the crest. All helmets had to be padded in order to fit correctly and to absorb shock from a blow.

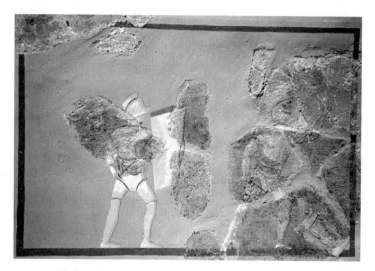

*Gladiators on a wall painting (photo by Carole Raddato)*

Helmets with their lining glued in place were generally only suitable for a few individuals, but by using arming caps of some kind, a wide range of people could use the same helmet. The complete, surviving examples from Pompeii weighed between 3.3 kg and 6.8 kg with an average weight of around 4 kg.

The introduction of visored gladiatorial helmets occurred at about the same time as Roman cavalry started to use face-mask

*Essedarius ('charioteer')*
- Armour: none
- Special feature: using British light chariot
- Period: Imperial
- Common opponent: *essedarius; retiarius*

helmets during their sports contests known as the *hippike gymnasia*. Besides offering protection for the face, and adding a certain intimidating impression to the opponent, both types of helmet may have added an additional challenge for the wearer by reducing their field of vision. Thus, by using visored helmets, the heavier gladiators acquired a handicap that their lighter opponents lacked.

Depictions (wall paintings, mosaics, lamps and metal figurines) reveal that some gladiators wore elaborate crests or plumes on their helmets some (but not all) of the time, in much the same way that soldiers did. It all added to the sense of spectacle, as well as serving to enhance the height (and therefore magnificence) of a gladiator and help to intimidate their foe.

## Breastplates

Although in the heyday of gladiatorial combat little in the way of body armour was worn, it is found amongst Republican gladiators right up to the time of Augustus. A relief in the Glypothek in Munich shows two gladiators, one triumphant, the other defeated, both wearing finely depicted sets of scale armour (*lorica squamata*). The *cardiophylax* ('heart protection') or partial breastplate was quite common and worn by the *provocator* and *thraex* amongst others. The protection offered by such armour was rudimentary and could even be argued merely to be token. Just as helmets had to be lined, so armour required some form of padding to make it effective by helping to dissipate the force from any blow. We know that both felt and leather undergarments were used for this purpose.

## Greaves

Greaves (*ocreae*) were designed to protect the lower leg. They were generally only used on the left leg, since it was this foot

*Gladiator painted on a glass vessel (photo by Shizhao)*

that was advanced when in the 'at the ready' stance, with the shield advanced and the sword drawn back ready to strike. Normally made of a copper alloy (bronze or brass), a greave had to have a fabric or leather liner to absorb shock when they were struck with a blade (or even kicked!), as well as straps around the calf to hold them in place. A possible military greave lining of leather is known from Vindonissa in Switzerland. Shorter gladiatorial greaves left the knee exposed (since it would usually be concealed behind the shield), but were arched over the foot, and were of two lengths (generally reflecting the size of the shield used). Longer ones provided some protection for the knee and could weigh between 2.2kg and 2.5kg each. Feet were left completely unprotected by greaves and thus remained vulnerable.

The examples from Pompeii were decorated with both embossed and engraved ornament. One pair depicts Neptune centrally on one shin and Jupiter on the other, with engraved

*Laquearius ('ceiling-maker')*
- Armour: shoulder guard
- Special feature: lasso, spear
- Period: Imperial
- Common opponent: *arbelas; essedarius; murmillo; secutor*

tendrils surrounding them. Another pair is covered in embossed mythological scenes, whilst a short example depicts a triumphant gladiator holding aloft a palm branch, the sign of his victory.

Greaves were used by the Roman army during the Republican period and were reintroduced during the early 2nd century AD in some regions. They were subsequently employed by Roman cavalry in their games known as the *hippika gymnasia*, but invariably providing protection for the knee, which cavalrymen – unlike gladiators with large shields – needed.

## Armguards

Just as with greaves, a metal armguard (*manica*) could be used by both gladiators and infantry. Although no known gladiatorial examples survive, a number of military examples have been excavated and they are now understood in some detail. They were articulated on three or four leather straps that ran the full length of the defence internally. A series of curved steel or brass plates were riveted to the straps which overlapped upwards (from the wrist to the shoulder) when worn on the sword arm. This ensured that, when the sword arm being held horizontally was struck by a blade, the blow was deflected towards the inside of the elbow, where the plates naturally bunched together and so were at their thickest. If worn on the left arm (as would a *retiarius*) then they might overlap downwards. The defences are sometimes depicted with multiple straps or laces hanging loose, suggesting that they may be ties for securing the armour to the wearer's limb.

Another form of *manica* that was depicted was made up of overlapping scales, just like the scale body armour worn by soldiers. No example of such a scale armguard has yet been identified amongst the archaeological material, even though scales are common finds on military sites. However, such a defence is shown in use on the Borghese mosaic, its grey colour indicating either steel or tinned copper alloy scales. Many *manicae* , both scale and plate, are also shown with a body strap attached to the top of the armguard, presumably to prevent the defence from sliding down, out of position. To be effective, like all armour, the armguard would have to have been worn over padding of some kind.

## Shoulderguards

Replacing a shield for a *retiarius*, there was a shoulderguard (traditionally identified as the *galerus*, although the evidence for this term is slim at best). This rested at the top of the left arm and afforded the wearer some protection for his face. When combined with an armguard, it offered protection similar to that of a shield but allowed a *retiarius* to hold his trident two-handed if he so wished. They were curved at the top as well as turned outwards, to prevent the wearer hitting his head and also deflect blows outwards. Surviving examples from Pompeii are decorated with various embossed motifs, including in one case a bust of Hercules and in another various nautical elements (a steering oar, anchor, trident, dolphin and crab!) recalling the supposed fishing origin of the *retiarius*. Used together with an armguard and padding, this would have made a good substitute for a shield. They weighed in the region of 1 kg and were 30–35 cm in height.

## Padding

As well as some padding under any armour, gladiators were also sometimes depicted wearing thick padding on their limbs. This was by no means universal, since it invariably involved a compromise between protection and manoeuvrability. There are no surviving examples, but mosaics and wall paintings are general a pale, creamy colour, suggesting they may have been from something like padded, undyed cotton. Straps or binding around the limbs held the padding in place.

## Shields

Several different types of shield were used by gladiators. One of the most familiar from reliefs, mosaics and frescoes, was the curved rectangular body shield also used by legionary troops. It not only provided excellent protection between the shoulder and knee, but could also be used as a weapon in its own right, punching with the metal boss or the upper rim, perhaps even slamming the lower rim down onto an opponent's foot.

An actual example of this type of shield, often known as a *scutum* (although the word actually refers to any type of shield), was excavated from the city of Dura-Europos in Syria, on the west bank of the Euphrates. The city served as a base for a Roman army unit during the 3rd century AD. The shield was shown to be made of three layers of wooden laths, the outer layers being glued horizontally and the middle one vertically, thereby using the grain of the wood to increase the protection offered. The outer face was painted with elaborate designs depicting scenes from the Trojan Wars, as well as bearing an image of a lion (a possible legionary badge) and winged victories with an eagle. Like nearly all Roman shields, it had a horizontal wooden handgrip. Modern reconstructions of the shields, which might have a brass or iron boss, weigh in the region of 7 kg.

*Retiarius and* secutor *on the Nennig mosaic (photo by Carole Raddato)*

Representations of gladiatorial shields of the curved, rectangular type suggest that these too were decorated on the front face. Most include right-angled *digamma* motifs in each of the four corners and these are sometimes depicted on legionary shields too. They do not feature the thunderbolts and eagle wings found on legionary shields, however, with abstract designs appearing instead.

Small circular shields (*parmae*) were also used by some types of gladiators, including *equites, hoplomachi* and *thraeces*. Some may have been made of wood but a convex example with a rim excavated from Pompeii, 0.37 m in diameter, was made of metal and decorated with two concentric laurel wreaths in low relief around a central repoussé boss of silver, which represented a head of Medusa. It weighed just 1.6 kg and closely resembles a miniature version of a Greek hoplite shield so may have belonged to a *hoplomachus* gladiator.

The distinction between the two types of shield – large rectangular (*scutum*) and small circular (*parma*) – led to a certain factionalism amongst followers, with adherents of the two types known as *scutarii* and *parmularii*. This was true for *murmillo/thraex* and *murmillo/hoplomachus* contests in particular. It may have reflected the fact that the gladiator with the smaller shield was placed at a disadvantage and was thus inevitably an underdog when facing an opponent with the larger shield.

## Props

One type of gladiator, the *pontarius*, required a piece of apparatus for their performance: the *pons* or bridge. No examples survive, merely rather crude representations, but it seems to have been made of timber and comprised a platform with ramps at either end. A *pontarius* then piled his rocks on the platform and could hurl them at his attacking opponents.

Other scenery was used for themed conflicts, where groups of fighters were set against each other in recreations of major battles from the past (particularly those Rome had won). However, these were normally fought by condemned criminals, rather than true gladiators from the gladiatorial schools, whose battles were usually one-on-one, minimalist affairs.

## The *armaturae*

The different types of gladiator were known as *armaturae*. We know from the Roman military writer Vegetius that the *armatura* was the type of drill performed by a soldier (or gladiator) according to the type of equipment with which he had been issued. This means that *armaturae* were less about how gladiators were equipped (and minor differences within the same type can be found), but rather how they actually fought. The whole point of such a wide range of *armaturae* was to provide variety for audiences. Whilst some stock pairs were used (*retiarius* v. *secutor*, *eques* v. *eques* and so on) mixing other types could be interesting, particularly when matching a left-handed gladiator with a right-handed one.

## Andabata

The *andabata* (the name may be Gallic in origin) was a type of gladiator who fought blind, either because they were blindfolded or because they wore helmets with no eye holes. They seem to have been paired together. Their purpose seems to have been to provide comedic value, as they staggered around trying to find their opponents. However, they do not seem to have been very common, which may have been part of the novelty, although they were sufficiently well known for Cicero to joke about them.

## Arbelas

The *arbelas* is only mentioned once in a single literary source and does not occur in any inscriptions but is shown on several reliefs wearing scale armour, but this may well be the Greek name for a *contraretiarius*, since they seem to have been paired with the *retiarius*. The key element was that, like the *dimachaerus*, the *arbelas* fought shieldless and wielded a gauntlet a with semi-circular blade on his left arm and *arbelas* may well have been just another name for the *scissor*. According to Artemidorus, as with a man who dreamed of fighting as a *dimachaerus*, one who dreamed of being an *arbelas* would marry a wife who was a poisoner, ugly, or malicious.

## Bestiarius

Those who performed such hunts were known as *bestiarii*, or men who fought animals, although they were sometimes also

*Murmillo ('little fish')*
- Armour: helmet, greave, armguard, curved rectangular shield
- Special feature: short sword
- Period: Imperial
- Common opponent: *retiarius; thraex; hoplomachus*

known as *venatores* (hunters). Indeed, there seems to have been as much confusion over the difference between the two in ancient times as there is now. Confusingly, a handler of such animals who prepared them for the arena might also be known as a *bestiarius*. Sculpted reliefs of the Republican period show fully armed gladiators fighting wild animals but, by the Imperial period, *bestiarii* fought with a spear and no armour, although some padding might be used on the left arm. The poet Martial describes a *bestiarius* called Carpophorus who achieved fame by killing a bear, a lion and a leopard. One particular variant of combat against wild animals was what is now known as *taurocatapsia* or bull-wrestling, first exhibited at the games by Julius Caesar. A man would quite literally wrestle a bull to the ground, starting off on horseback and leaping onto the beast.

*Bestiarii* were generally held in lower esteem than 'proper' gladiators and they baffled the Christian writer Cyprian:

> What state of things, I pray you, can that be, and what can it be like, in which men, whom none have condemned, offer themselves to the wild beasts – men of ripe age, of sufficiently beautiful person, clad in costly garments? Living men, they are adorned for a voluntary death; wretched men, they boast of their own miseries. They fight with beasts, not for their crime, but for their madness. (Cyprian, *To Donatus* 7)

The Emperor Domitian established a training school not far from the Colosseum for *bestiarii* (one of four gladiatorial schools he set up) known as the *Ludus Matutinus*.

## *Crupellarius*

We have only one reference to the type of gladiator known as a *crupellarius* and that comes in Tacitus' account of the revolt of Florus and Sacrovir in AD 21. The Gallic revolt associated with these two men was associated with the tribes of the Treveri and Aedui respectively. Florus was quickly defeated by the Romans in the Ardennes with the help of his fellow Treveran, Iulius Indus, a Roman cavalry commander, but the Aedui under Sacrovir proved a tougher nut to crack. Finally meeting the Romans in battle to the north of Autun, their forces included slaves armed as gladiators, described by Tacitus as *crupellarii*, 'clad after the national fashion in a complete covering of steel', going on to note that 'though they were ill-adapted for inflicting wounds, they were impenetrable to them'. The legionaries' swords could not penetrate their armour, but the ever-resourceful Roman army soon found a solution,

> snatching up hatchets and pickaxes, hacked at their bodies and their armour as if they were battering a wall. Some beat down the unwieldy mass with pikes and forked poles, and they were left lying on the ground, without an effort to rise, like dead men. (Tacitus, *Annals* 3.46)

Our understanding of the *crupellarii* would end there, were it not for a small statuette from Versigny in France which some scholars believe might represent just such a gladiator. The figure wears a large, cylindrical helmet with a distinctive nasal protrusion and small holes, presumably for ventilation, resembling the great helm of a medieval knight rather than the familiar types of gladiatorial helmet. His limbs, shoulders and upper torso bear incisions suggestive of segmental armour of the type worn by Roman legionaries.

Tacitus is very clear that this was a Gallic type of gladiator, perhaps meaning that it was only ever seen in Gaul itself, which might explain the Romans' evident surprise at encountering these heavily armoured men in the field and the lack of any other references to them.

## Dimachaerus

This gladiator's name literally means 'two swords' in Greek and thus provides the vital piece of information we need to know – the *dimachaerus* fought shieldless with a second blade in his left hand

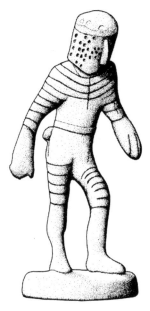

*Statuette of a* crupellarius *(drawing by M. C. Bishop)*

instead. This was a particular novelty for the Romans who were used to all swordsmen fighting with both a blade and a shield. According to Artemidorus, a man who dreamed of fighting as a *dimachaerus* would marry a wife who was a poisoner, ugly, or malicious.

## Eques

The *eques* (cavalryman) was a gladiator who generally fought on horseback, but could dismount if needed. A mosaic in Madrid shows two *equites* fighting dismounted. They were armed with a spear, carried a round shield in their left hand and had a full-face visored helmet with a brim with a pair of plumes, one on either side of the helmet bowl. Unusually, they wore a tunic and not just the *subligaculum*. *Equites* were often used to open the gladiatorial part of a *munus*, once the *prolusio* was over. According to Artemidorus, any man who dreamed of competing as an *eques* would end up with a wife who was both noble and rich, but not very intelligent.

## Essedarius

*Essedarii* were charioteers, supposedly based on the British chariots Julius Caesar encountered in 55 and 54 BC and which Julius Agricola found again during his campaigns in Scotland under Domitian. Such chariots were extremely light vehicles, designed for speed and manoeuvrability. Artemidorus believed that a man who dreamed of fighting as an *essedarius* would marry a woman who was lazy and stupid (presumably because the charioteer did not bother to dismount in the arena and they had the reputation for being rather dim).

## Female gladiator

The word *gladiatrix* is a modern invention and was unknown to the Romans. Female gladiators were known but fought in one of the known *armaturae*, rather than being a specific type in its own right.

## Gaul

The *Gallus* (normally translated as 'Gaul', but it also means 'cockerel', 'priest of Attis' and 'reaping machine' – there was potential for humour if nothing else) was another type of gladiator derived from a particular nationality. Gauls had a particular significance for the Romans, partly because they had attacked Rome in 390 BC, according to tradition (there are complicated reasons for disputing the date). Little is known about the equipment of the *Gallus* – they may have been equipped like Gallic nobility and worn helmets and mail shirts, carried a large shield, and wielded a long sword, but it is also possible that they fought like ordinary warriors, naked but for the shield and sword. The type had largely disappeared by the Augustan period.

## Hoplomachus

The *hoplomachus* was effectively a Roman gladiatorial tribute to the hoplite of classical Greece. Equipped with a small circular shield, a spear and probably at least some body armour, they were similar to Samnites. They would have been slow and cumbersome, but well-protected and, importantly, with a greater reach than a sword-armed opponent.

## Laquearius

The *laquearius* is thought by some to have been a variant of the *retiarius*, perhaps even a novelty act. Instead of a net, they were equipped with a lasso.

## Murmillo

The *murmillo* (or *myrmillo*) was originally the chief opponent for the *retiarius*. but could also be found fighting the *thraex*. The name, which comes from a small, salt-water fish, played upon the appearance of *retiarius* as a kind of fisherman. They were equipped with a helmet, armguard, rectangular shield and a greave. They were found from the 1st to the 3rd centuries AD. Festus recorded a taunt supposedly levelled at a *murmillo* by a *retiarius*:

Equites *fighting on foot (photo by Carole Raddato)*

A *retiarius* fighting against a *murmillo* chanted 'Why do you flee, Gaul? I'm after the fish, not you!', because the *murmillo* fought with Gallic weaponry and because *murmillones* used to be Gauls, with a depiction of a fish on the helmet. (Festus 358 L)

## Paegnarius

The *paegnarius* was to some extent an entertainment act, rather than a 'serious' gladiator. Lacking armour, they were protected with just padding on the left arms and equipped with whips or canes. They seem to have been more akin to slapstick comedy than combat to the death.

## Pontarius

The *pontarius* ('bridge man') was a variant of the *retiarius*. A rectangular wooden platform with ramps at either end was provided for the *retiarius*, together with a supply of rocks instead of a net. His opponent, a *murmillo* or *secutor*, then tried to assault the ramp under a hail of stone. Such a scene is depicted on a relief from Kos in Greece showing the *retiarius* Kritos and his assailant Mariskos. The relief is damaged on one side so it is possible there was a second attacker on the other ramp. This is suggested by a barbotine-decorated pot from Lyon showing a trident-armed *pontarius* called Scorpus fending off two attackers (Flamma and Februarius) with rocks.

## Provocator

The *provocator* ('challenger') was equipped in much the same way as the *murmillo*, with a helmet, rectangular shield, armguard and greave. Inscriptions mentioning *provocatores* are known from Rome (Anicetus and Pardus), Pergamum (Nympheros) and Pompeii (Mansuetus). The type was known in the 1st century BC, as is clear from a passage from Cicero:

> ... as the fact is that this band did not consist of men picked out of those who were for sale, but of men bought out of jails, and adorned with gladiatorial names, while he drew lots to see whom he would call Samnites, and whom *provocatores*, who could avoid having fears as to what might be the end of such licentiousness and such undisguised contempt for the laws? (Cicero, *For Sestius* 64.134)

Some *provocatores* seem to have worn a small breastplate (*cardiophylax*) protecting the upper chest at the front and held in place by straps, visible on the back. It is generally held that they only ever fought other *provocatores* but this assertion is difficult to prove.

## Retiarius

The *retiarius* ('net man') first appears under the Empire. Armed only with a trident, a net and a knife, he was lightly armoured, wearing only a shoulderguard and armguard most of the time. His only clothing was the loin cloth and ankle bindings. Using

*Paegnarii (photo by Carole Raddato)*

speed to both evade and tire his opponent, he would cast his net in an attempt to snare or trip up the more heavily armoured gladiator lumbering after him.

Occasionally, a *retiarius* would fight in a tunic, in which case he was known (unsurprisingly) as a *retiarius tunicatus*!

> A Gracchus fighting, not indeed as a *murmillo*, nor with the round shield and scimitar: such accoutrements he rejects, indeed rejects and detests; nor does a helmet shroud his face. See how he wields his trident! And when with poised right hand he has cast the trailing net in vain, he lifts up his bare face to the benches and flies, for all to recognise, from one end of the arena to the other. We cannot mistake the golden tunic that flutters from his throat, and the twisted cord that dangles from the high-crowned cap; and so the pursuer who was pitted against Gracchus endured a shame more grievous than any wound. (Juvenal, *Satires* 8.199–210)

*Secutor ('pursuer')*
- Armour: helmet, greave, armguard, curved rectangular shield
- Special feature: short sword
- Period: Imperial
- Common opponent: *retiarius*

There is some suggestion (largely innuendo in Juvenal's *Satires*) that such *retiarii* were viewed as effeminate.

Although the origins of the *retiarius* are often assumed to have been in fishing (despite the fact that fishermen would tend to use a net or a spear, but seldom both), it has been pointed out that they may have had a more martial origin. In 332 BC, the inhabitants of the island city of Tyre used tridents and nets to defend themselves against the siege mounted by Alexander the Great.

A skull from the gladiator cemetery at Ephesus shows the result of a fatal blow from a trident. The spacing of the horrendous wounds exactly matches that of the tines of surviving tridents.

The earliest depictions of a *retiarius* – on glass vessels from Lyon dating to the late 1st century BC – shows a man with a net and trident not only wearing greaves but also, apparently, body armour. A marvellous 2nd century AD pot from a grave in Colchester depicts a *retiarius* called Valentinus appealing for clemency, having been defeated by the *secutor* Memnon. A 3rd-century AD mosaic from Spain shows events from a fight between a *secutor* Astyanax and the *retiarius* Kalendio, who is marked with a Θ (theta) to show that he lost and was killed.

*Gladiators on pottery from Colchester (photo by Carole Raddato)*

The classic opponents for the *retiarius* (or *contraretiarii*, as they were known) were the *murmillo* and, later, the *secutor*, both of whom appear to have specialised in fighting the net man. *Retiarii* were the principal gladiator type to fight from a makeshift platform known as a 'bridge' (*pons*), in which case they might be described as a *pontarius*. Here they substituted their speed (and their net) for a height advantage and, by way of compensation, it seems, a pile of rocks for throwing at their would-be assailants!

Artemidorus was of the opinion that dreaming of being a *retiarius* meant a man's wife would be both poor and apt to wander (because the *retiarius* depended on moving around a lot and was of comparatively low status even amongst gladiators).

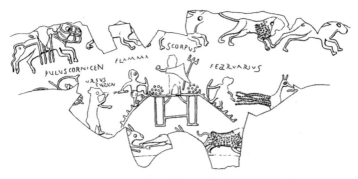

Pontarius *in action (drawing by M. C. Bishop)*

## Sagittarius

The *sagittarius* was an archer, equipped with the recurved composite bow. To achieve maximum efficiency with this weapon (both in terms of rate of shooting and accuracy), an archer needed to practise all their lives, so a gladiator who adopted this *armatura* could never be as proficient with the composite bow as a native from a region where it was used who had grown up with the weapon.

## Samnite

The Samnite (*samnis*) was one of the earliest types of gladiator. They owe their origins to the Samnite Wars which Rome fought against the inhabitants of Samnium during the second half of the 4th century BC. Samnites fought with the *gladius* and carried the curved, rectangular body shield. They normally wore a greave on the left shin and had some form of protection on the sword arm, either padding or a metallic armguard. On their head they wore a broad-brimmed helmet with a visor that completely covered the face. There is a record of an early Samnite in the 2nd-century BC writer Lucilius:

In the public show given by the Flacci was a certain Aeserninus, a Samnite, a nasty fellow, worthy of that life and station. He was matched with Pacideianus, who was by far the best of all the gladiators since the creation of man. (Lucilius, *Satires* 2.172–5)

## Scaeva

The left-handed gladiator (*scaeva*) was a novelty act that flew in the face of the normal style of hand-to-hand combat. Romans (and, indeed, nearly every body else in the ancient world) fought with a sidearm (some form of sword or spear) in their right hand and a shield in their left. When joining the army, for instance, those who were naturally left-handed had to retrain to be right-handed. The whole point of left- versus right-handed combat was that it challenged both fighters to think laterally if they hoped to win.

It is clear that a *scaeva* was not really a specific *armatura* in its own right, but rather a subdivision of the standard *armaturae*. Hence Commodus boasted on an inscription of being a *secutor* of the *primus palus* who also fought left-handed, whilst a funerary inscription from Sorrento describes a '*mirmillo*'(!) as a *scaeva* and a graffito from Pompeii depicts a man called Albanus fighting with his shield in his right hand and sword in his left with the abbreviation SC (for *scaeva*).

## Scissor

The *scissor* seems to have been another name for the *arbelas*.

## Secutor

The *secutor* ('pursuer' or 'follower', pl. *secutores*) was the standard opponent for the *retiarius*, chasing him relentlessly around the arena. The name was a joke on the personal assistants of

Roman officials who followed them around closely. The *secutor* was generally depicted armed with the classic short sword and protected by a helmet, a curved rectangular shield, an armguard on the sword arm and a greave on the shield leg. The helmet had two simple eye holes, a small neck guard and a curving front-to-back crest. Its smooth shape made it hard for the trident to gain purchase and left little upon which the net could snag. It was the Emperor Commodus' favourite *armatura* and he was allegedly named *primus palus* of the *secutores* 620 times. A mosaic from Rome (now in the Museo Arqueológico Nacional in Madrid) shows the *secutor* Astyanax triumphing against the *retiarius* Kalendio, despite being covered by his opponent's net. Artemidorus wrote that any man who dreamed of fighting as a *secutor* would marry a woman who (on the plus side) was both attractive and rich, but (at the other extreme) proud and disdaining her spouse (indicating that *secutores* had high status amongst gladiators, but were a bit too vain).

## Thracian

The Thracian (*thrax* or *thraex*) was another of the earliest types of gladiator, originating with captives from Rome's wars at the beginning of the 1st century BC. The type was said to have been introduced to the arena by Sulla. Equipped with a small circular or square shield, their principal weapon was a sword with a curve or angle in it (*sica*). They wore a broad-brimmed helmet with a protective visor and limb protection, usually a greave on the left shin and an armguard or padding on their sword arm. Those who fought as a Thracian did not necessarily need to come from Thrace itself – Exochus (see above, p.53) was from Alexandria in Egypt. According to Artemidorus, a man who dreamed of fighting as a *thraex* would marry a wife who was rich (because of all that armour), crafty (the angled blade) and fond of being first (due to the Thracian method of advancing).

Secutor *versus* retiarius *(photo by Carole Raddato)*

## Veles

The *veles* is assumed to have been a light-armed gladiator, although no details about this *armatura* survive. *Velites* were the light skirmishers of the early Republican legion and, as such, missile-armed troops with little in the way of armour. The gladiatorial *veles* was apparently similar and they fought each other with spears.

## Venator

Hunting was very popular in Roman society and was a regular way of supplementing the normal diet with slightly exotic game. It seems to have been one of the chief pastimes of bored soldiers on Hadrian's Wall, dedicating altars to hunting deities. It is no surprise, then, that this was carried over into the arena with staged wild beast hunts performed by huntsmen (*venatores*). It might

*Astyanax defeats Kalendio*

not seem like much of a spectator sport to us, but observing the finer points of how a hunt was managed may have engaged a crowd almost as much as watching duelling gladiators. There was also the chance of an unexpected yet gory end for either the animals, the hunter, or possibly even both.

On the same piece of pottery that depicts a *pontarius*, there is a fragmentary hunting frieze with hares and boar in the lower register. Elsewhere, scenes with hounds are shown, suggesting that a different set of skills were being demonstrated by *venatores* than those of the *bestiarii* fighting against exotic big game.

## Support staff

Rather bizarrely, the actual combat might be accompanied by musicians on wind instruments (the straight *tuba* and the curved *cornua* are shown on reliefs and mosaics) and an organist on a water organ (*hydraulis*). Parts of the *hydraulis* dated to the 3rd century AD were found at Aquincum (Budapest in Hungary) as well as piece of two examples from Pompeii. These, together with surviving descriptions, help us

*Musicians playing organ and horn (photo by Carole Raddato)*

to understand how the instrument worked. It evidently made an impressive sound, as the poet Claudian attests, describing the playing of the organist:

> Him too whose light touch can elicit loud music from those pipes of bronze that sound a thousand diverse notes beneath his wandering fingers and who by means of a lever stirs to song the labouring water. (Claudian, *Panegyric on the Consulship of Manlius Theodorus* 339–42)

In the Imperial period, once a contest was finished, and if there was a corpse to dispose of, then a man dressed as Charun, the Etruscan demon of death (not to be confused with Charon, the ferryman, who carried the dead across the River Styx), entered the arena. He tested to see if the deceased really was dead, finished them off with his mallet if not, and then dragged off the offending remains. Tertullian referred to him obliquely as 'the brother of Jupiter', which amongst the Roman pantheon would mean either Neptune, god of the sea, or Pluto, the god of the underworld (the latter obviously equivalent to Charun). Some of the skulls from the gladiator cemetery at Ephesus showed possible signs of impact by such a hammer.

Finally, the arena could then be smoothed out and bloodied sand replaced by the *harenarii* or arena attendants (usually slaves).

## The arenas

The word arena comes directly from the Latin word for sand, *harena* (the Romans were as prone to dropping aitches and adding them unnecessarily as readily as anybody else). This was because, wherever gladiators fought, they did so on sand. Since most, but not all, gladiators chose to fight barefoot, this not only made for a less painful surface than stone or wood, but it also had the advantage of soaking away any spilled blood. The specialised gladiatorial venues with which we are now so familiar – oval amphitheatres – were actually a comparatively late development. As mentioned earlier, the first public performances were mounted in the Forum Boarium and Forum Romanum in Rome, and later chariot racing circuses and theatres were used to stage fights between gladiators. As late as 43 BC, Cicero proposed reserving space around a statue of the late Servius Sulpicius Rufus on the Rostra for his descendants so that they could watch 'games and gladiators'. By the early Imperial period, another repurposed open space, the Saepta Iulia (located next to the Pantheon in Rome), was being used for gladiatorial shows. Designed as the voting area for Roman citizens, it was exploited by both Augustus and Gaius.

At Ephesus (Turkey), the theatre, only some 900m south-west of the gladiatorial cemetery, contains graffiti demonstrating the presence there of gladiators, and the same secondary use is found for theatres at Athens, Aphrodisias, Assos and Hierapolis. Similarly, the stadium at Ephesus was also used for gladiatorial contests, a small arena being inserted in its eastern end when it was no longer used for athletic contests. In Rome, the oldest chariot racing stadium, the Circus Maximus, was also exploited for gladiatorial shows but was particularly popular for wild beast shows, since it provided much more room than amphitheatres or theatres.

Moreover, even when amphitheatres did begin to appear, they were at first temporary structures of wood and catastrophic collapses like that described above under Tiberius were not unknown. The word *amphitheatrum*, which literally means 'all-round theatre', was used to describe an oval structure with banks of seating that completely surrounded the arena. Whilst a theatre was a true semicircle, the oval shape of an amphitheatre was very carefully laid out using geometrical principles and was not simply two semicircles joined together. The earliest stone amphitheatre was not in Rome but at Capua, although that was replaced by the surviving structure in the Imperial period. This means that the earliest surviving stone amphitheatre is in the small provincial town of Pompeii and that only dates back as far as *c.*70 BC, with the foundation inscription referring to it as a *spectacula* and not an *amphitheatrum*. It measured 135 m by 104 m overall, with the arena 67 m by 35 m dug into the ground by about 2 m (spoil being used for the earthen banks under the seating). The arena was surrounded by a wall more than 2 m high which was decorated with frescoes, including hunt scenes. Pliny the Elder believed that the first amphitheatre ever was that built in 52 BC by Scribonius Curio to celebrate gladiatorial games for his dead son. Clearly he was slightly wide of the mark in some respects, but it may well be that this was the first time such an oval structure was referred to as an *amphitheatrum*. The structure he described was actually two timber theatres hinged together which could be rotated to form an amphitheatre.

As the Roman empire spread, so did amphitheatres. The Roman army helped, since all legionary fortresses and even some auxiliary forts were equipped with an amphitheatre. The example at Caerleon in Wales, just outside the south-west gate of the fortress of the Second Legion Augusta, can still be visited. With its oval

*Pompeii amphitheatre inscription (photo by M. C. Bishop)*

*Caerleon amphitheatre (Crown Copyright)*

arena partially excavated below ground level, the spoil was then piled up to form the base for the seating embankments, reinforced with stone revetment walls. It was probably enhanced with a timber superstructure to provide sufficient seating for the whole legion. Although it was once thought that military amphitheatres were largely used for parades, scholars now believe they also served as venues for gladiatorial contests and animal hunts much like those in any provincial town. The presence of a shrine to Nemesis, the goddess of fate favoured by gladiators, in the amphitheatres at Caerleon and Chester only helps to confirm this.

At either end of the short axis of the arena, there was the *Porta Sanavivaria* (Gate of Life) on one side and the *Porta Libitinensis* (Gate of Death) on the other. Triumphant gladiators would leave through the former, whilst the figure dressed as Charun would emerge from the latter in order to remove the remains of the defeated. Beyond the *Porta Libitinensis* lay the *spoliarium*, the chamber where the dead were stripped and prepared for cremation or burial.

## The Colosseum

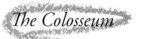

Undoubtedly, the best known of all the amphitheatres in the Roman world was the Flavian Amphitheatre, often called the Colosseum (a nickname it acquired from its proximity to a large statue of the sun god Helios that used to stand next to it). Built over the remains of the lake outside Nero's reviled Golden House, it was a masterpiece of Roman engineering and architecture. Covering an area of just 2.4 ha but capable of seating somewhere between 50,000 and 80,000 spectators (at a time when the population of Rome is thought to have been something under half a million), it was the largest custom-designed gladiatorial venue in the Roman Empire. By way of comparison, the nearby Circus Maximus, primarily designed for chariot races but (as just mentioned) also used for gladiatorial contests, was more than 7 ha in extent and could probably seat 150,000.

The substructures of the Colosseum housed ramps, machinery for moving scenery and lifts to hoist animal cages up into the arena, as well as cells for accommodating combatants and animals whilst they awaited their turn. There was also a large drain surrounding it, reflecting the fact that a large lake had been drained in order to construct the structure.

Ancillary structures in the vicinity of the Colosseum included four Imperial gladiatorial schools, one of which – the *Ludus Magnus* – is still partly visible. It included a small arena for practice (63 m by 42 m), surrounded by seating (so that enthusiasts could watch their heroes practise and perhaps size them up for betting purposes. There were cells around the periphery and it was linked to the main amphitheatre by means of a tunnel. The other schools, the *Ludus Mutatinus*, *Ludus Dacicus* and *Ludus Gallicus*, were also near the Colosseum. The complex also included a health centre (*sanitarium*) and morgue (*spoliarium*), a scenery store (*choragium*) and an armoury (*armamentarium*). Elsewhere, near the Baths of Trajan, there was a camp for members of the Classis Misenensis (the fleet based at Misenum on the Bay of Naples) who had responsibility for handling the awnings (*vela* – literally, 'sails' – that formed the *velarium* or awning) that served to shade the audience in the amphitheatre from the sun during performances. The remains of the apparatus for deploying the awning still survive on the exterior of the Colosseum. Lucretius described the colourful effect of such awnings at the theatre:

> The awnings, saffron, red and dusky blue,
> Stretched overhead in mighty theatres,
> Upon their poles and cross-beams fluttering,
> Have such an action quite; for there they dye
> And make to undulate with their every hue
> The circled throng below, and all the stage,
> And rich attire in the patrician seats.
> (Lucretius, *On the Nature of Things* 4.75–81)

In the Colosseum, as in all amphitheatres, social stratification was openly practised. The organiser of the games, whether the *editor* or an emperor, sat in a box on one of the long sides of the arena. The nobility sat next to the edge of the arena, just about far enough removed from any unpleasantness to be safe,

*Ludus Magnus remains (photo by M. C. Bishop)*

whilst behind them sat the bulk of the male population. Women and slaves were confined to the rearmost, upper tiers of seating (often added in timber, even in stone amphitheatres). The only exception made was for the Vestal Virgins, the celibate women priests who tended the sacred flame of the goddess Vesta in their circular temple next to the forum. It is they who are depicted in the front row of Gérôme's painting vigorously making the thumbs-down gesture. The rest of the women (and the slaves) thus had the advantage of being close to the awnings and the shade they provided, but the disadvantage of being far away from the action down in the arena.

Although construction of the Colosseum began in AD 72 under the Emperor Vespasian, funded by the spoils from his Jewish War, it was not finally dedicated until AD 80 under his son, the Emperor Titus, with a massive programme of games that allegedly lasted 100 days and saw the deaths of 5,000 animals. The poet Martial wrote a series of poems (*On Spectacles*) to commemorate the event and, although doubt has been cast upon their accuracy, the rich mix of mythology, ingenuity in dealing death and the sheer exotic variety of animals slaughtered was clearly designed to

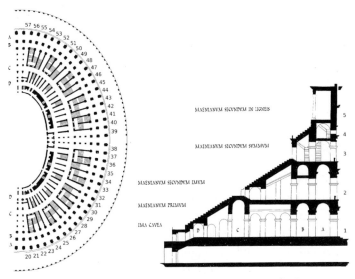

*Colosseum cross-section (drawing by M. C. Bishop)*

impress an audience who had probably become inured to routine gladiatorial combats and wild beast hunts. However, the poet only actually describes one gladiatorial combat between an equally matched pair and does not even mention their *armaturae*:

> While Priscus drew out, and Verus drew out the contest, and the prowess of both stood long in balance, oft was discharge for the men claimed with mighty shouts; but Caesar himself obeyed his own law: that law was, when the prize was set up, to fight until the finger was raised; what was lawful he did, oft giving dishes and gifts therein. Yet was an end found of that balanced strife: they fought well matched, matched well they together yielded. To each Caesar sent the wooden sword, and rewards to each: this prize dexterous valour won. Under no prince but thee, Caesar, has this chanced: while two fought, each was victor. (Martial, *On Spectacles* 29)

There was another imperial amphitheatre in Rome. The *Amphitheatrum Castrense*, so called because of its proximity to the camp of the Imperial horse guards, the *equites singulares*, was not in fact a military amphitheatre, but actually part of a palace complex constructed by Elagabalus (AD 218–22) in the early 3rd century AD. It was adopted by Constantine for his own private entertainment, sharing the spectacles staged there with only a few select guests.

## *Provincial amphitheatres*

Outside of Rome, Italian cities such as Verona and Capua routinely had an amphitheatre, but Puteoli on the Bay of Naples, because of its pre-eminent role as a trading port, built a second during the latter part of the 1st century AD.

Beyond Italy, and throughout the empire, amphitheatres could be found around most legionary fortresses, some auxiliary forts and most towns and cities. Provincial amphitheatres like those at Nimes, Arles (both France), Pula (Slovenia) or El Jem (Tunisia) were as magnificent as anything in Italy outside of Rome, although some of the more far-flung – in Britain, for example – were markedly less impressive, often small and constructed with earthen banks and timber, such as those outside the British towns of Cirencester or Silchester. The example at Dorchester was even a converted Neolithic henge monument. The similarity of the amphitheatre at El Jem (with its arena 65 m by 39 m) to the slightly larger Colosseum (77 m by 46 m) was one of the reasons it was chosen to stand in for its larger Italian cousin in the film *Gladiator* (with the aid of some digital enhancement).

In the Roman town of Carnuntum, which stretched between the modern villages of Bad Deutsch-Altenburg and Petronell in Austria, and which surrounded a Roman legionary fortress, an interesting discovery was recently made. It has long been known that Carnuntum had two stone amphitheatres, one for the fortress and one for the town, but geophysical survey has recently

### The army and gladiators

The Roman army not only enjoyed watching gladiators, but actually had a much closer connection with gladiatorial combat. In 105 BC, we find P. Rutilius Rufus importing specialist trainers for his army from the gladiatorial school of C. Aurelius Scaurus with the specific aim of improving his soldiers' sword skills. Soldiers were now to practice fencing against stakes and then against each other using blunted weapons. Soon after, the Roman general Marius used troops trained by those same gladiatorial trainers to defeat the Cimbri, so the system passed its first test.

This type of training became integral to the Roman army, not only when instructing new recruits, but also in maintaining the skills of even the most hardened veterans. Commanders regularly reviewed them and any shortcomings in drill would be noticed.

revealed the plan of a gladiatorial school closely resembling the *Ludus Magnus*. It had a circular, rather than oval, training arena, but its proximity to one of the amphitheatres leaves little doubt over its identification.

Amphitheatres were not confined to the western half of the empire and more than 20 are now known from the East. They were not as common as in the West and this was used in the past to suggest that the East was more 'civilised' and less enthusiastic about gladiators, but it is clear that this was not the case and the cemetery and theatre at Ephesus only serve to confirm this. It is, however, true that much of the terminology of gladiatorial combat was simply transliterated into Greek, the common language of the region. Only *gladiator* (which became *monomachos* or 'lone fighter') and *munera* (*philotimia* – 'the love of honour') were actually translated.

These all serve to confirm the universality of gladiatorial games (in the broadest sense) throughout the Roman Empire.

# CHAPTER 6

# LIFE AS A GLADIATOR

*I have seen men weighed down by bodily exercise, and carrying
about the burden of their flesh. Rewards and wreath crowns are
set before them, while those who judge them cheer them on — not
to deeds of virtue, but to rivalry in violence and discord.
The one who excels in giving blows is crowned.*

Tatian, *Address to the Greeks* 23

## Recruitment

NEARLY ALL GLADIATORS WERE SLAVES OWNED by a *lanista* who
was, effectively, their manager. In the case of Imperial gladiators,
they were of course owned by the emperor, who had his own
*lanista* in the *Ludus Magnus* and the other *ludi* to manage them.
The *lanistae* then made money by hiring out their fighters for
games and this was duly taxed by the government (and the cost
of that tax passed on to customers). It has been estimated that
the tax brought in between 60 and 120 million sesterces per
annum to the Imperial treasury. Moreover, if a top gladiator was
killed in the arena, the *editor* of the games would be required
to compensate the *lanista* (who had obviously made a sizeable
investment in his fighter, not only in their purchase cost, but in

their training and upkeep) for as much as 50 times the fee for which the gladiator had been hired. Gladiators represented big money, whether it be for those holding the games, the *lanistae* or the government raking in the tax.

Those gladiators who were indeed slaves were selected according to their looks, physique and general good health. They had often been captured during warfare, sold to a *lanista* by a former master or condemned in court to a gladiatorial training school (*condemnatio ad ludum gladiatorium*). Either way, they joined a *ludus* or training school, usually named after the *lanista*, such as the *ludus Aemilius* mentioned by Horace or the *ludus Neronianus* at Capua. *Lanistae* were not highly thought of, Seneca comparing them to pimps, although Cicero saw nothing wrong with his friend Atticus buying a *ludus*, complete with gladiators, noting that he could earn back his investment after just two shows. Gladiators within such a training school would then be described as belonging to a *familia*, such as the *familia gladiatoria* or *familia venatoria*.

There is some evidence that at least some gladiators adopted stage names, the obvious examples being the two female gladiators, Achillia (a female version of Achilles, the great Greek warrior) and Amazon (the Amazons fought on the side of the Trojans against the Greeks in the Trojan War). Their Trojan-War-themed soubriquets are too obvious to have been their real names and the coincidence of them being paired together frankly implausible. This may have been quite a popular theme. Astyanax, depicted on the Madrid mosaic, was named after the son of Hector (the Trojan hero). Other mythological names occur: Meleager on the Borghese mosaic recalls the hero of the same name, famed for hunting the Calydonian Boar. Talamonius on the same mosaic is a Romanisation of Telamon, who was also on the boar hunt, whilst Bellerefons is clearly Bellerophon, who captured Pegasus, the winged horse. Other names, like Hilarus ('jolly') on a Pompeian graffito, are regular Greek slave names. The graffiti from Pompeii record the exploits of the match between

Marcus Attilius and Lucius Raecius Felix, whose names suggest they were Roman citizens (or, at the very least, freedmen). Stage names were not universal then, so may have been preferred by owners or perhaps even the gladiators themselves.

There were some men who, having achieved their freedom for some reason, opted to stay on as freedmen gladiators (there is obviously the suspicion here that they may have become institutionalised during their time in a *familia gladiatoria*). Occasionally, there were also Roman citizens who decided to fight in the arena for whatever reason (known as *auctorati*). There was in fact a legal process (known as *auctoratio*) whereby a free man who fancied a career in the arena would get permission from a tribune of the people and then contract himself to a *lanista* or even directly to the *editor* of the games (as a form of freelance gladiator). One man even treated his *lanista* like a pawnbroker, selling himself more than once, only to have his sister bale him out each time; she put a stop to this by cutting off his thumb (rendering him useless for the arena) and he duly sued her! Cicero scoffed at Marc Antony's brother for choosing to fight as a gladiator occasionally. Vitellius, one of the unlucky three in the so-called Year of the Four Emperors (AD 69) explicitly forbade members of the equestrian order (the second rank of nobility) from doing this (suggesting that some had been doing it):

> Strict measures were taken to prevent Roman equestrians from degrading themselves in gladiatorial schools and the arena. Former emperors had driven equestrians to such actions by money or more often by force; and most municipal towns and colonies were in the habit of rivalling the emperors in bribing the worst of their young men to take up these disgraceful pursuits. (Tacitus, *Histories* 2.62)

It had indeed amused Caligula to force equestrians and even senators to fight, but there was a world of difference between what an autocrat compelled men to do and what they chose to do voluntarily, and any Roman could see that. There were certainly few faster ways of earning the disapproval of all strata of society than by volunteering to fight as a gladiator, so like the Emperor Commodus, they must have wanted to do it really badly. When Marcus Aurelius expressed doubts about a former gladiator wanting to hold public office, the man observed that he had seen many members of the senate fight in the arena in his time.

At this point, it is important to distinguish true gladiators from the *noxii* or condemned men who were to be executed in the arena, sometimes by fighting each other, sometimes fighting wild animals, but generally providing entertainment during the lunchtime hiatus, between the animal hunts of the morning and the gladiatorial shows of the afternoon. These *noxii* might include prisoners of war amongst their numbers, as well as run-of-the-mill criminals, particularly after major campaigns. They were not, however, members of the gladiatorial schools, did not participate in the regular training that marked a gladiator, nor was there any subtlety in the contest. It was simply pitiless slaughter.

Although most gladiators were indeed slaves, there were free men who felt drawn to participate for whatever reason, as has just been mentioned. However, it was not just men, but women too who were found in the arena. A relief sculpture and inscription from Halicarnassus (Turkey) records the *missio* or discharge of the two female gladiators mentioned above, Amazon and Achillia. They are both shown in the 'at the ready' stance, without helmets but with the rectangular shields and *gladii* of *murmillones*.

The poet Juvenal brought up the subject of female gladiators in his sixth *Satire* focused on women:

> Who has not seen one of them smiting a stake, piercing it through and through with a foil, lunging at it with a shield, and going through all the proper motions? A matron truly qualified to blow a trumpet at the Floralia! Unless, indeed, she is nursing some further ambition in her bosom, and is practising for the real arena. What modesty can you expect in a woman who wears a helmet, abjures her own sex, and delights in feats of strength? Yet she would not choose to be a man, knowing the superior joys of womanhood. What a fine thing for a husband, at an auction of his wife's effects,

*Amazon and Achillia, female gladiators (photo by Carole Raddato)*

to see her belt and armguards and plumes put up for sale, with padding that covers half the left leg; or if she fight another sort of battle, how charmed you will be to see your young wife disposing of her greaves! Yet these are the women who find the thinnest of thin robes too hot for them; whose delicate flesh is chafed by the finest of silk tissue. See how she pants as she goes through her prescribed exercises; how she bends under the weight of her helmet; how big and coarse are the bandages which enclose her haunches; and then laugh when she lays down her arms and shows herself to be a woman! Tell us, you grand-daughters of Lepidus, of the blind Metellus, or of Fabius Gurges, what gladiator's wife ever assumed accoutrements like these? When did the wife of Asylus ever gasp against a stake? (Juvenal, *Satires* 6.247–67)

Of course, this was satire, so it is exaggerated and part of the amusement value inevitably comes from the fact that it evidently concerned a noble woman who was indulging her taste for gladiatorial combat by participating in it herself. We know that there were female gladiators but this need not be seen as evidence that they were all of noble birth. However, Juvenal's satire derived its bite from having a core of truth to it. Under Nero, Tacitus records the following for the year AD 64:

> The same year witnessed a number of gladiatorial shows, equal in magnificence to their predecessors, though more women of rank and senators disgraced themselves in the arena. (Tacitus, *Annals* 15.32)

This became a cause of concern for the Roman authorities, but it was not until the reign of Septimius Severus that a stop was put to women participating in gladiatorial combat. The principal problem lay not in women fighting in the arena, but in the low social standing of gladiators in society reflecting unfavourably upon noble Roman women.

In September 2000, on an otherwise quiet news day, the Museum of London chose to publicise the fact that remains found during excavations at Great Dover Street in Southwark, south of the Thames, may have been those of a female gladiator. It was, if so, the first such burial ever recorded. The body had been cremated over a pit, into which the remains of the pyre and the body had collapsed (a *bustum* – remember, gladiators were first known as *bustuarii*). Grave goods included incense burners, some lamps (one showing a gladiator) and the remains of food (including doves and chickens, figs, dates and almonds), possibly a meal for the afterlife. Roman cremation was often not very efficient, and analysis of fragments of the pelvis of the skeleton suggested that it had belonged to a woman in her twenties. Of course, it is impossible to be certain that this woman really was a so-called gladiatrix, but it remains a possibility.

Before they entered service, all gladiators took an oath of loyalty (*sacramentum*) to their *lanista*. We know its approximate wording from writings by both two of Nero's courtiers, Petronius (his so-called Arbiter of Taste) and Seneca (his adviser), who both paraphrase it:

We took an oath to obey Eumolpus; to endure burning, bondage, flogging, death by the sword, or anything else that Eumolpus ordered. We pledged our bodies and souls to our master most solemnly, like regular gladiators. (Petronius, *Satyricon* 117)

The words of this most honourable compact are the same as the words of that most disgraceful one, to wit: 'Through burning, imprisonment, or death by the sword.' From the men who hire out their strength for the arena, who eat and drink what they must pay for with their blood, security is taken that they will endure such trials even though they be unwilling; from you, that you will endure them willingly and with alacrity. (Seneca, *Letters* 37.1–2)

The precise wording is unknown, but these two texts indicate it must have been something along the lines of 'I promise to endure burning, bondage, flogging and death by sword to obey my master'.

# Training

The relationship between military and gladiatorial training has already been alluded to. The late Roman writer Vegetius preserves an account of the training of new legionary recruits which he specifically compares to the gladiatorial system:

The ancients, as is recorded in the books, trained recruits in this way. They wove rounded shields of wicker like basketry, in such a way that the frame should be double the weight of a battle shield. And likewise they gave the recruits wooden foils, also double weight, in place of swords. And next they were trained at the stake, not only in the morning, but also in the afternoon. For the use of stakes is particularly advantageous not only for soldiers but also for gladiators. And neither arena nor field ever proved a man invincible in arms, unless he was carefully taught training at the stake. However, single stakes were fastened in the ground by each recruit, in such a way that they did not wobble and protruded for

*Training at the stake (photo by J. C. N. Coulston)*

six feet. The recruit practised against this stake with the wicker shield and singlestick as though with a sword and shield against an enemy; so, he might aim for the head or face, then he is threatened from the sides, then he strained to cut down at the hams and shins; he retreated, attacked, leaped in, as if the enemy were present; he assaulted the stake forcefully, fighting skilfully. In doing this, care was taken that the recruit rose up in this way in order to wound, but did not lay himself open to a blow anywhere. (Vegetius, *De Re Militari* 1.11)

A surviving relief from Milan shows a gladiator with just such a stake (*palus*), in this case cheekily topped by his gladiatorial helmet so that his face could be seen. The use of double-weight dummy weapons was considered extremely important by the Romans, the intended effect being that once used to the heavy practice weapons, the real thing would seem extremely light when they came to use it. The fact that both the army and the gladiatorial schools used this method of training for hand-to-hand combat clearly indicates that they felt it worked.

Gladiators were taught by an instructor (*doctor* – our word doctor comes from the Latin *doctor medicinae*, instructor in medicine) in much the same way as the *campidoctor* instructed soldiers – the *campus* was the practice ground where Roman soldiers trained, the very first being the Campus Martius in Rome. Usually experienced gladiators, these *doctores* seem to have specialised in one of the *armaturae*. There is a *doctor retiariorum* known from Cordoba (Spain), a *doctor murmillonum* from Concordia and Rome (both in Italy), a *doctor hoplomachorum* and a *doctor thraecum* from Rome, as well as a more general *doctor gladiatorium* from Cologne in Germany.

One of the principles drummed into soldiers was the need for constant training and this would have been essential for gladiators too. There will have been variations adapted to the different *armaturae* (so it might be supposed that the *retiarius*, for instance, under the direction of a *doctor retiariorum*, practised stabbing at the stake with his trident, as well as throwing his net at it). The next stage on from the stakes for the more experienced was mock combat with live opponents and Onasander described how this was done for soldiers:

> Next after dividing the army into two parts he should lead them against each other in a sham battle, armed with staves or the shafts of javelins. (Onasander, *Strategicon* 10.1.4)

Although we lack any surviving tactical manuals for gladiatorial combat, we can reconstruct something of the way in which gladiators fought. Gladiators were taught a standard 'at the ready' stance which was shared with Roman legionaries and which is depicted on a variety of media. This consisted of achieving a comfortable, balanced position, with the left foot forward and the shield covering the left side whilst the right foot was kept back with the sword held horizontally by the side. This explains why, when only one greave was worn, it was worn on the left side. Gladiators with large shields were then protected from their helmeted head to their greave-clad shin. When the gladiator wished to strike with the sword, it was necessary to change balance by advancing the right leg and bringing the sword arm into play. At this point their armguard served to protect the advanced sword arm from any blow against it.

Various types of blow were possible with the *gladius* (and other swords), although some seem to have been favoured over others at different times and perhaps even at the same time by different instructors. There is some evidence that the various possible moves were known as *numeri* ('numbers') or *dictata* ('rules'), a character in Petronius' *Satyricon* disliking a Thracian who fought by the rules (*ad dictata*), whilst Julius Caesar expected recruits to his gladiatorial school to learn the *dictata*. Clearly there was a fine balance between knowing the rules and sticking too closely to them. First was the horizontal stab (*punctim*) which could easily be delivered from the 'at the ready' stance and could be fatal with just one blow. Next came the chop (*caesim*), which required the arm to be raised and was thus more suited to use in the midst of close combat. Finally, there was a variant of the *punctim* which required reversing the grip on the sword and stabbing downwards with the blade as if it were a dagger and this, again, was only suitable in certain circumstances, notably close combat. The design of the *gladius*, with a top nut holding the pommel onto the tang, suggests one more way in which it could have been used offensively, namely punching down with it onto the unprotected head of an opponent, so particularly suited when, say, a *secutor* was fighting a *retiarius*.

Whatever the weaponry, a great deal of attention must have been given to showmanship and this was where the manner in which the weapon was used would have mattered. The military writer Vegetius describes how deadly the tip of the *gladius* could be, observing that in some areas of the body a wound only needed to be 2 Roman inches (49 mm) deep to be fatal. This was good for soldiers in battle but made for a poor show in the arena, where spectacular (but not fatal) wounds would make for a longer, more interesting contest. At the same time, gladiators who let a contest go on too long ran the risk of displeasing the crowd if they grew bored, so knowing how to to use a weapon effectively, and where the key vulnerable points of the body were, was of paramount importance.

The combination of skill, training and art are all cited by Cyprian, a Christian writer deploring gladiatorial contests:

> ... if you turn your eyes and your regards to the cities themselves, you will behold a concourse more fraught with sadness than any solitude. The gladiatorial games are prepared, that blood may gladden the lust of cruel eyes. The body is fed up with stronger food, and the vigorous mass of limbs is enriched with brawn and muscle, that the wretch fattened for punishment may die a harder death. Man is slaughtered that man may be gratified, and the skill that is best able to kill is an exercise and an art. Crime is not only committed, but it is taught. What can be said more inhuman – what more repulsive? Training is undergone to acquire the power to murder, and the achievement of murder is its glory. (Cyprian, *Epistles* 1.7)

Training in the Imperial schools lasted at least six months before achieving the lowly status of *tiro*. The effects of all this training could be seen on the skeletons of gladiators from the cemetery at Ephesus. The average height of the men examined was in the region of 1.68m. By comparing the dimensions of bones found with 'normal' examples that might be expected, it was possible to see how the enhanced musculature of the gladiators left its mark on their skeletons. This was true not only in their joints, but also in the calf, thigh and upper arm.

## The contest

Shows were advertised well in advance, summarising what might be expected on the programme, as well as extra luxuries (such as *vela erunt* or 'there will be awnings') to tempt the undecided. Advertisements (*edicta munerum*) were painted on walls, with the names of the sponsors the most prominent of all.

*Adverts for games from Pompeii*

From Decimus Lucretius Satrius Valens, permanent priest of Nero Caesar, son of Augustus, twenty pairs of gladiators, and Decimus Lucretius Valens, his son, ten pairs of gladiators will fight at Pompeii on 27th April; there will be animal hunts and awnings. [signed] Polybius (*CIL* IV, 7995)

An impression, albeit fictional, of the sort of spectacle advertised and then put on at Pompeii can be gained from Petronius:

> Just think, we are soon to be given a superb spectacle lasting three days; not simply a troupe of professional gladiators, but a large number of them freedmen. And our good Titus has a big imagination and is hot-blooded: it will be one thing or another, something real anyway. I know him very well, and he is all against half-measures. He will give you the finest blades, no running away, butchery done in the middle, where the whole audience can see it. And he has the wherewithal; he came into thirty million when his father came to grief. If he spends four hundred thousand, his estate will never feel it, and his name will live for ever. (Petronius, *Satyricon* 45)

The night before a contest, the gladiators of a *familia* enjoyed a banquet known as the *cena libera* ('free meal'). Bizarrely, to our

Spectators attending gladiatorial games needed **tickets** in the form of a pottery or bone token (*tessera*) to gain entry. These could be obtained for free beforehand, or queued up for on the day of the contest, and bore a sector, row and seat number (e.g. CVN II GRAD III LOC VII would be *cuneus* (sector) 2, *gradus* (row) 3, *locus* (seat) 7). Some of the sector numbers can still be seen above entrances to the Colosseum. Programmes (*libelli*) could be purchased telling audience members what to expect from the day's entertainment and which gladiator was to fight which opponent.

eyes at least, it was freely accessible and members of the public were allowed in to gawp. It has been speculated that the origins of the meal may have lain in the sacrificial nature of the original funerary gladiatorial contests, but by the Imperial period, it was as much a part of the spectacle as the combat itself. It was also one of the few times when gladiators had the opportunity to eat something other than barley and beans (Plutarch noting the fare was good but the gladiators were not interested in it).

The games began with a procession (*pompa*) where all the competitors could be seen and admired, along with the animals and prisoners involved in providing the entertainment. Such parades are depicted on some reliefs. An example of what it might have looked like in a provincial town comes from Pompeii and shows a pair of toga-clad lictors carrying the *fasces*, bundle of rods containing an axe, that symbolised a magistrate (different ranks of magistrates had differing numbers of lictors). Next came three trumpeters (*tubicines*, playing the *tuba*), who were later to provide the music to accompany the events, and then a platform (*ferculum*) bearing two statues, carried by four bearers. Next were figures carrying a plaque (*tabella*) and a palm branch. Then comes a man who is probably the *editor*, the person responsible for mounting the games. He is followed by six more men carrying the gladiators' shields and helmets. Another man is carrying something that looks like a bowl and he is followed by another musician playing a *lituus*. Finally there are two men leading horses. The gladiators themselves do not appear in the relief, although they were obviously an important part of the procession, particularly since, unhelmeted, their public would be able to see them in all their glory. In Rome itself, *pompae* would have been larger and more magnificent.

After the *pompa* came the main events. A pattern was established for the games by the time of the Empire. The broad outline was always the same: the morning would be devoted to animal hunts, with a lunchtime interval generally consisting of the execution of criminals, before the main event – the gladiatorial matches – started.

The animal displays were first up in the morning and there were three ways they could have been presented, any or all of which might have been applied. By the Imperial period, crowds had long ago grown bored with just seeing exotic animals moping around and now needed some form of interaction, and the bloodier the better. The first option might be to have one type of animal pitted against another, such as lions against elephants. A second was for *bestiarii* or *venatores* to be pitched against them. Finally, there was what might be called execution by wild animal (for those suffering *damnatio ad bestias* as it was known), a fate traditionally associated with Christians, although it was not exclusively reserved for them, nor is it thought to have been as common as some supposed.

Although the philosopher (and tutor to Nero) Annaeus Seneca is often cited as having been against the gladiatorial games in a famous passage, he was in fact protesting about these lunchtime executions, as is clear from the fact that those who had been condemned to the arena (*damnatio to ludum*), unlike gladiators, were unprotected:

> By chance I attended a mid-day exhibition, expecting some fun, wit, and relaxation – an exhibition at which men's eyes have respite from the slaughter of their fellow men. But it was quite the reverse. The previous combats were the essence of compassion; but now all the trifling is put aside and it is pure murder. The men have no defensive armour. They are exposed to blows at all points, and no one ever strikes in vain. Many persons prefer this programme to the usual pairs and to the bouts 'by request'. Of course they do; there is no helmet or shield to deflect the weapon. What is the need of defensive armour, or of skill? All these mean delaying death. In the morning they throw men to the lions and the bears; at noon, they throw them to the spectators. The spectators demand that the slayer shall face the man who is to slay him in his turn; and they always reserve the latest conqueror for another butchering. The outcome of every fight is death, and the means are fire and sword. This sort of thing goes on while the arena is empty. (Seneca, *Moral Letters* 7.3–4)

After these so-called *meridionali*, the gladiatorial component of the show would be started off with a little light sparring between men using practice weapons, to pique the interest of the audience. This taster of things to come was known as the *prolusio* or prelude. Before there could be any serious fighting, however, there had to be an examination of the weaponry (a process known as *probatio armorum*) to make sure the weaponry (*ferra acuta* – literally, 'sharp steel') was acceptable.

The gladiatorial contests themselves thus occurred in the afternoons and were normally confined to just one pair at a time. There was a rule that the pair should be equally matched and not of the same *armatura* (so *thraex* could not fight *thraex*, nor *retiarius* another of his kind), although there was an exception insofar as *eques* was always matched against *eques*. There was a good reason for this: any more than one pair at a time could actually detract from the enjoyment of the audience, who prided themselves on being able to judge the finer points of a match and most of whom would have been firm followers of some of the more famous combatants from particular gladiatorial schools. To understand why more than one pair was not a good idea, imagine being in the audience at a giant football stadium with several games going on at once. The exception to this was when teams were pitted against each other, such as the occasion recorded by Suetonius:

> Once a band of five *retiarii* in tunics, matched against the same number of *secutores*, yielded without a struggle; but when their death was ordered, one of them caught up his trident and slew all the victors. Caligula bewailed this in a public proclamation as a most cruel murder, and expressed his horror of those who had had the heart to witness it. (Suetonius, *Caligula* 30.3)

Such team events might be billed as re-enactments of famous battles. After the excitement (and death) of the morning hunt and lunchtime interval executions, the first pair of gladiators would enter the arena. These were usually *equites*, a pair of mounted gladiators. Unless they already knew them, this was the audience's first chance to size them up. They would be hard task masters: they would expect them to get on with it, for there not to be too much running away and certainly no reluctance to actually engage in combat. At the same time, nobody (except perhaps the occasional gladiator) wanted to see it all over as fast as possible. It was, after all, a contest, and the crowd would want to see a stylish, technical fight, and the best of all would be one closely balanced. The pairings were ultimately decided by the individual sponsoring the games (the *editor*). Cicero, who was not averse to using the term 'gladiator' as an insult, could understand the concept of a stylish performance and would cheerfully employ it as a metaphor to make a point:

> For as we see athletes, and in a similar manner gladiators, act cautiously, neither avoiding nor aiming at anything with too much vehemence, (for over-vehement motions can have no rule), so that whatever they do in a manner advantageous for their contest, may also have a graceful and pleasing appearance; in like manner oratory does not strike a heavy blow, unless the aim was a well-directed one;

nor does it avoid the attack of the adversary successfully, unless even when turning aside the blow it is aware of what is becoming. (Cicero, *Orator* 228)

At the crucial moment in the struggle between two opponents, when one managed to land a telling blow, the crowd would cry '*Habet! Hoc habet!*' or 'he's had it!'. The victim, if still capable, might then decide to appeal to the crowd for mercy by dropping his shield and raising the forefinger of his right hand. This is the gesture most commonly shown in contemporary representations, rather than the famed thumb gesture. If the contest was indecisive and both contestants were dismissed, they were said to be *stantes missum* ('dismissed standing'); alternatively, they might pause for a break and then carry on. Indeed, it was sometimes mandated that a fight should carry on *ad digitum*, in other words until one or other contestant pleaded for mercy. Depending upon how the crowd then responded – and there were clearly many factors affecting such a decision, such as loyalty, appreciation of both technique and style and perhaps even whether they had got out of bed on the wrong side that morning – with the famous *pollice verso* ('turned thumb') gesture mentioned by Juvenal that is the very quintessence of gladiatorial combat: thumbs up or down. Cries of '*Iugulum!*' ('kill him!') from the onlookers might be matched by appeals of '*Mitte!*' ('let him live!').

The most commonly believed version of the *pollice verso* gesture sees the thumbs-up to mean 'let him live' and thumbs down 'kill him'. However, it has been suggested that the thumbs-up gesture (with phallic undertones) meant 'kill him' and the thumbs down implied 'spare him' (thumbs up not acquiring a positive meaning until comparatively recently). The outcome of the less-favourable version of the gesture is shown on relief sculpture and in mosaics, but who had made that decision? There is some evidence to suggest that it was up to the victor and that all the audience (and even the *editor*) could do was appeal to that individual's generosity. Of course, an appeal for clemency from the emperor was probably not something one would overlook lightly.

The lucky loser whom the crowd judged had fought well would enjoy *missio* and be allowed to live to fight another day. Those who were not so lucky faced execution by the victor. A relief from Lucus Feroniae (Italy) shows one Republican-period gladiator, sword blade resting on his right shoulder, finishing off another with his dagger. Another relief depicts a kneeling gladiator, his face concealed behind a shield apparently attached to his head, about to be executed by the man who had defeated him.

Each contest was overseen by a *summa rudis* ('top stick') who acted like a referee in a modern boxing match. These individuals can be seen on depictions of gladiatorial combats wielding a long cane and, perhaps understandably, are most visible when one gladiator is down and appealing for mercy. He was supported by a deputy, the *secunda rudis*. It was up to the *summa rudis* at this point to ensure fair play and stop either of the contestants taking unfair advantage of the pause in proceedings. A tombstone from Amisus in Turkey records how a bent referee managed to turn a result and the victor, Diodorus, ended up dead as a result. The tombstone of *summa rudis* Publius Aelius from Pergamum records that he had honorary citizenship from a number of cities in the East – Abdera (Greece), Apros (Kermeyan in Turkey), Bizye (Vize in Turkey), Larisa (either in Greece or Turkey), Nicomedia (İzmit in Turkey), Perge (Turkey), Philippopolis (Plovdiv in Bulgaria), Thasos (Greece), Thessalonica (Thessaloniki in Greece) – suggesting that he was an itinerant umpire.

If the umpire thought the gladiators were not trying hard enough, he might use his cane to encourage them to produce a better performance. He would doubtless have been sensitive to the mood of the crowd. Where there was a decisive winner, then they would be awarded a palm branch, a laurel crown and perhaps a purse of coins or other gifts as a sign of their victory from the *editor* of the games. Prize money was divided between

*Pompeii graffiti including a gladiator appealing (drawing by M. C. Bishop)*

the gladiator and his *lanista*: Marcus Aurelius set the amount for the gladiator at 25% of the purse if free, 20% if a slave.

When the time came to leave, the crowd did so by means of the exits known as *vomitoria*. Although the word *vomitorium* is often thought to be a room where debauched Roman diners could shed what they had been eating earlier to make room for more, this is in fact a myth. *Vomitoria* were exits from arenas which were carefully designed so that they did not constrict a crowd in a hurry to leave a building.

## Career

The hardest part of a gladiator's career was making the move from an untried *tiro* (new recruit) to a man who had survived (and possibly even won) his first fight. Experienced gladiators were known as veterans (*veterani*) and the number of their victories was

*Summma rudis on the Zliten mosaic (photo by Carole Raddato)*

recorded, since it is found associated with their names on both graffiti and tombstones. Once a gladiator had started winning, beyond surviving, they could aspire to reaching the status of *primus palus*, 'first stake', named after the stake against which they trained. The best gladiator in the school would be *primus palus*, the next best *secundus palus* and so on. There is evidence for at least four grades and inscriptions from the East suggest that there may have been up to eight levels. When viewed in the context of the legislation of AD 177 to limit the costs of games using the ranks of gladiators, this suggests that all gladiators within a school would thus have had a *palus* ranking, not just an elite few. Inherent in the system seems to have been the ability for any gladiator to work their way up through the hierarchy, although how many (or what proportion of) victories were necessary to achieve this is unclear.

Whilst the ultimate goal of most gladiators was retirement, that does not mean that some of them at least did not enjoy what they did and look forward to a fight:

> Even among the gladiators of Caesar (the Emperor) there are some who complain grievously that they are not brought forward and matched, and they offer up prayers to God and address themselves to their superintendents intreating that they may fight. (Epictetus, *Discourses* 1.29.37)

*Gladiator with palm branch (photo by Carole Raddato)*

## Collegia

Like many groups in Roman society, gladiators organised themselves into trade guilds, even though they were only slaves, for the most part. It is generally assumed that *collegia* acted as burial clubs, but they probably acted as social clubs too. Elsewhere in Roman society, *collegia* organised feasts as a component of religious festivals and gladiatorial guilds may have helped organised the *cena libera* before a fight. *Collegia* were organised into *decuriae* ('tens') and, if they were big enough, *centuriae* ('hundreds') and headed by *initiales* ('leaders' or 'founders'). An example was the *collegium* of Silvanus recorded on an inscription from Rome dating to AD 177 when Marcus Aurelius and Commodus were co-emperors:

> For Emperor Caesar Lucius Aurelius Commodus and Marcus Plautius Quintillus consuls, the *initiales* of the *collegium* of Silvanus

Aurelianus, *curatores* Marcus Aurelius Hilarus, freedman of the emperor, and Coelius Magnus, *cryptarius*.

**decuria I**

Borysthenes, *thraex* veteran
Clonius *hoplomachus* veteran
Callisthenes *thraex* veteran
Zosimus *essedarius* veteran
Plution *essedarius* veteran
Pertinax *contraretiarius* veteran
Carpophorus *murmillo* veteran
Crispinus *murmillo* veteran
Pardus *provocator* veteran
Miletus *murmillo* veteran

**decuria II**

Vitulus *murmillo* veteran
Demosthenes armguard-maker
Felicianus *retiarius* beginner
Servandus *retiarius* beginner
Iuvenis *murmillo* sword-maker
Ripanus *contraretiarius* beginner
Silvanus *contraretiarius* beginner

Secundinus *provocator* beginner
Eleuther *thraex* beginner
Pirata masseur

**decuria III**

Barosus *contraretiarius* beginner
Aemilianus *contraretiarius* newly arrived
Ulpius Euporas Proshodus *contraretiarius* beginner
Aurelius Felicianus (?civilian)
Aurelius Felix (?civilian)
Zoilus civilian
Flavius Marissus (?civilian)
Flavius Sanctus (?civilian)
Diodorus civilian

**decuria IIII**

Aprilis *paegniarius*
Zosimus *thraex* sword-maker
(*CIL* VI, 631)

The likely burial function of the *collegium* is reflected by the post of *cryptarius*, the man who looked after the burial plot. It is noticeable how all of the veterans were in the first *decuria*, the beginners in the second and assorted other statuses in the third and fourth *decuriae*. Likewise, there were sword- and armourmakers, as well as a masseur. Presumably, all of the gladiators in the *collegium* belonged to the same *familia*, but this is not stated. It is known that there was a *collegium* for *summa rudes* in Rome since a tombstone of one of its members, Publius Aelius, is known from Pergamum (Turkey).

# Retirement

A gladiator who survived to retirement was awarded with freedom and the wooden sword or *rudis*, which was of course the

Rudis *from Saalburg (photo by C. Rusalen)*

very practice weapon with which they had trained. It is unclear whether this would have been an actual double-weight wooden sword, or whether it might in fact have been a symbolic replica, such as the slightly scaled-down wooden swords excavated from Carlisle (UK) and Saalburg (Germany). The wooden *sica* from the Roman fort at Oberaden mentioned above may have served a similar purpose for a *thraex*.

A successful gladiator, who had in most cases been a slave, might receive their freedom, enabling them to set up in business or (certainly in the turbulent Late Republican period) perhaps get into the security trade, acting as a politician's henchman. They might even aspire to the role of *lanista* and train other gladiators.

Even after retirement, it might be possible to persuade a gladiator to fight again for a very special occasion. The Emperor Tiberius offered a massive fee of 100,000 sesterces to *rudiarii* ('men who have received the *rudis*') who would fight in a games in honour of his grandfather Drusus.

## Life, health and death

Gladiators were expected to eat healthily as well as train in order to maintain peak fitness. Cyprian alludes to this in his Christian diatribe against the games:

> The body is fed up with stronger food, and the vigorous mass of limbs is enriched with brawn and muscle, that the wretch fattened for punishment may die a harder death. Man is slaughtered that man may be gratified, and the skill that is best able to kill is an exercise and an art. (Cyprian, *Letter to Donatus* 1.7)

*Paegnarius ('play fighter')*
- Armour: padded left arm
- Special feature: whip or cane
- Period: Imperial
- Common opponent: *paegnarius*

Analysis of the bones from the gladiator cemetery at Ephesus (Turkey) confirms that they enjoyed a special diet and showed just how much it differed from that of the general population. They apparently had a vegetarian diet (called *sagina* or 'stuffing'), preferring carbohydrate over protein. Gladiators were indeed nicknamed *hordearii* ('barley boys') and Galen notes that they mainly ate bean soup and barley, sometimes served as a pudding, sometimes watered down as a drink. However, aside from leading to excessive flatulence, barley and legumes could not provide everything they required for peak fitness and Galen made efforts to improve the diet of the gladiators under his charge at Pergamum. It has even been suggested that, to avoid calcium deficiency, gladiators consumed a special concoction which scientists believe was made from the ashes of burnt plants. This would ensure that their calcium levels were not just maintained but markedly higher than that of the general population. It has been speculated that one effect of this diet may have been to increase the subcutaneous body fat of the combatants, making it possible for them to receive fairly impressive-looking wounds without it having too much direct impact on their ability to fight. Cicero repeatedly plays on the word 'gladiator' in his Third Philippic speech against Julius Caesar's former right-hand man, Marc Antony, as a way of both sneering at his slightly thuggish physique and demeaning his status.

One of the paradoxes of the Roman world was that, apart from the very wealthy, those whose lives were most at risk (such as soldiers and gladiators) had access to some of the best living conditions (relatively speaking) and the highest quality healthcare. The physician Galen, whose writings were highly influential upon medieval medicine, began work as the doctor (*medicus*) for a gladiatorial school in Pergamum from AD 158 to 161 before becoming the personal physician of the Emperor Marcus Aurelius. He was clearly good at what he did, since his predecessor had lost 60 gladiators under his charge, whereas Galen only lost two. As he was treating the living and patching together the wounded, he was learning about anatomy, dissection of humans no longer being popular amongst the medical profession of his time.

Galen described treating an *eques* who had suffered a nasty wound to his thigh (an occupational hazard for any mounted warrior) and how he went about stitching it back together. Learning on the job, Galen's knowledge of drugs and how to use them slowly improved and he evidently diligently sought the correct treatments.

Again, skeletal analysis of the remains of 68 individuals from the gladiator cemetery at Ephesus has proved extremely informative with regard to the injuries and wounds they received. Most of those wounds were to the head and usually fatal, although a diamond-shaped puncture wound resembling the cross-section of a *gladius* blade showed signs of healing, whilst the triple puncture characteristic of a *retiarius*' trident was decidedly fatal. Others had been finished off with a blow to the head with a hammer, doubtless dealt by the figure dressed as Dis Pater or Charun. Some healed wounds to the head, it was suggested, may have resulted from over-vigorous training sessions.

We even have a joint epitaph with a medical twist from one of the training schools in Rome:

Claudius Agathocles, *medicus* of the emperor, physician at the *Ludus Matutinus*, made this for himself, Claudius the *lanista* of the emperor, Primitivus, keeper of the morgue, and Thelesphorus the *retiarius*, may the earth rest lightly upon you. (*CIL* VI, 10171)

Like everybody else in the Roman world, gladiators were usually concerned to make some sort of provision for a memorial once they were dead. At Ephesus, not only do many of the gladiators' tombstones survive, but there is also a gladiator cemetery which has been examined archaeologically. Scientific analysis of the bodies of some of the deceased has produced a wealth of extremely interesting information about the lives and deaths of the gladiators buried there.

# Accommodation

True to the notion of the *familia gladiatoria*, gladiators usually lived together in some form of barracks. Various *ludi* in Rome and elsewhere with practice arenas and cells for accommodation have already been mentioned but two sets of gladiatorial accommodation are known from Pompeii. The first, which apparently dated back to the beginning of the Imperial period, was a peristyle courtyard structure in Regio V of the town known as the House of the Gladiators. Excavated at the end of the 19th century, it was found to include over 100 graffiti connected with gladiators, recording Thracians, *murmillones*, *retiarii*, *equites* and *essedarii*. However, it was badly damaged in the earthquake of AD 62 and the barracks was moved to the *quadriporticus* next to the Triangular Forum in Regio VIII, which was uncovered in the 18th century. There were rooms on two floors around the central courtyard, the *lanista* having rooms on the upper floor whilst the gladiator cells were at ground level. There was even a kitchen with mess hall for communal dining and, on its wall, somewhat enigmatically, was written the name of Lucius Annaeus Seneca, that critic of at least some aspects of the games. When the building was first excavated, the remains of eighteen individuals were found including, in one cell, the skeleton of a woman wearing jewellery, lying next to the remains of a man; this poignant scene has invited many different interpretations over the years. The barracks also produced a number of pieces of gladiatorial armour – including helmets, greaves, belts, daggers, a shield and a spear – as well as graffiti attesting to the presence of the gladiators.

# Family

Apart from their *familia gladiatoria*, some gladiators had time to have their own families. Once they had retired and gained their freedom, they were of course able to do this, although it is possible that some were able to develop long-term relationships whilst still in service. The presence of a baby in a basket in one of the rooms of the *quadriporticus* might be interpreted as an indication that families were present there too. However, the unusual circumstances surrounding the eruption of Vesuvius, with people fleeing all over the city, provides no guarantees that bodies were found where they normally lived.

A number of inscriptions record family members of gladiators. Some are coy about the nature of the relationship:

> For the immortal shades, Marcus Ulpius Felix, retired *murmillo*, lived 45 years, member of the Tungrian nation, Ulpia Syntyche, freedwoman, and son Justus, set this up for her sweetest, well deserved. (*CIL* VI, 10177)

Others were more open:

> For the immortal shades, for Publicia Aromata, most loved wife, Albanus, a retired *eques* from the *Ludus Magnus*, she lived 22 years 5 months and 8 days, 3 feet in width by 8 feet in length (*CIL* VI, 10167)

Both of these men were described as retired from service. Even in the case of memorials which do not explicitly mention that a

*Gladiator graffiti from Pompeii (drawing by M.C. Bishop)*

gladiator was retired it is not possible to be sure that they were married whilst in service, or even that the term 'wife' or 'husband' was used in anything other than an unofficial capacity:

> For the immortal shades, Glaucus, from Mutina, fought in seven combats, killed in the eighth, lived 23 years and 5 days, Aurelia and his friends (set this up) for a deserving husband. I advise you to follow your own star, not to trust Nemesis, and be deceived as I was. Hail and farewell. (*CIL* V, 3466)

One gladiator, commemorated on a stone from Milan and dead whilst still in service, had been with his wife, presumably as fellow slaves, since the age of 15 and left a five-month-old daughter:

> To the immortal shades, for Urbicus, a *secutor*, ranked *primus palus*, from Florentia, fought 13 times and lived 22 years, his daughter Olympias, whom he left aged 5 months, and Fortunensis, his daughter's (slave?), and his wife [*uxsor*] Lauricia (set this up) for her well-deserving husband, with whom she lived for 7 years. I warn you: kill whomever you defeat. His followers will take care of his shade. (*CIL* V, 5933)

There is, within this sad text, a hidden tale: the warning suggests that one of those opponents Urbicus defeated during his career fought him again and did not repay the debt. There are many more pathetic epitaphs like this, but wives and lovers must

*Gladiator barracks at Pompeii (photo by M. C. Bishop)*

always have known the risks involved in being a gladiator and that the odds were not good.

## Fans

Gladiators were every bit as popular as modern sports stars. Specific named warriors were celebrated on a variety of media. A particular type of mould-blown glass cup found in the north-western provinces of the Empire appears to celebrate a troupe of gladiators. With a frieze running round the cup showing pairs of gladiators, each with their name above them – Spiculus and Columbus, Calamus and Hories, Petraites and Prudens, and Proculus and Cocumbus – this was obviously the ultimate piece of merchandising. In Britain, examples of this type of vessel are known from Colchester, Dorchester, Gloucester, Leicester, London and Wroxeter and have been dated to the middle of the 1st century AD. Graffiti from Pompeii praise particular gladiators by name, whilst detailed sketches of favourite fights are known, incorporating brief summaries of the results. Names were accompanied by letters: V stood for *victor* (winner, often accompanied by a Roman numeral denoting the number of successful combats), M for *missus* (lost but spared), whilst P meant *periit* (died) and L *libet* (freed). Even large-scale mosaics (like that from the Villa Borghese in Rome) name individual gladiators, possibly the favourites of whoever commissioned the pavement in the first place. Other depictions of gladiators on lamps and on tableware such as samian may have been bought as souvenirs.

Passions were often high at the games and in AD 62 a serious riot broke out at Pompeii between the inhabitants of the town and visitors from Nuceria. The Roman historian Tacitus describes what happened:

> About the same date, a trivial incident led to a serious affray between the inhabitants of the colonies of Nuceria and Pompeii, at a gladiatorial show presented by Livineius Regulus, whose removal from the senate has been noticed. During an exchange of raillery, typical of the petulance of country towns, they resorted to abuse, then to stones, and finally to steel; the superiority lying with the populace of Pompeii, where the show was being exhibited. As a result, many of the Nucerians were carried maimed and wounded to the capital, while a very large number mourned the deaths of children or of parents. The trial of the affair was delegated by the emperor to the senate; by the senate to the consuls. On the case being again laid before the members, the Pompeians as a community were debarred from holding any similar assembly for ten years, and the associations which they had formed illegally were dissolved. Livineius and the other fomenters of the outbreak were punished with exile. (Tacitus, *Annals* 14.17)

Deprived of their games, the inhabitants of Pompeii were probably greatly relieved when the ban was lifted three years later, after the earthquake of AD 62.

Other passions could be aroused too. There was definitely something about gladiators that meant their followers could

*Gladiators on a moulded glass vessel (photo by Carole Raddato)*

*Borghese gladiator mosaic*

*Gladiators on a lamp (photo by Carole Raddato)*

*Gladiators on samian ware (photo by Carole Raddato)*

take their enthusiasm to extremes. In his sixth *Satire*, Juvenal tells the story of Eppia, a senator's wife who ran off with a gladiator:

> And what were the youthful charms which captivated Eppia? What did she see in him to allow herself to be called 'a she-Gladiator'? Her dear Sergius had already begun to shave; a wounded arm gave promise of a discharge, and there were sundry deformities in his face: a scar caused by the helmet, a huge wen upon his nose, a nasty humour always trickling from his eye. But then he was a gladiator! It is this that transforms these fellows into Hyacinths! it was this that she preferred to children and to country, to sister and to husband. What these women love is the sword: had this same Sergius received his discharge, he would have been no better than a Veiento. (Juvenal, *Satires* 6.103–13)

Even the audience at a gladiatorial contest might take the opportunity to indulge in some opportunistic flirting, despite women being banished to the upper tiers of seating by Augustus. That could not stop the exchange of meaningful glances in smaller amphitheatres.

*Fresco of the riot at Pompeii (photo by M. C. Bishop)*

## Status

For some, gladiators were the lowest of the low; for others, they were stars to be admired. Cicero showed his utter contempt for Catiline after his failed coup by disparagingly referring to him in his *Against Catiline* speech as a 'gladiator' and throughout Roman writings this same lack of respect is to be found (as has already been mentioned, he used the same insult in his speeches against Marc Antony repeatedly). The fact that gladiators ate barley would not have helped – the Roman army only issued barley to animals or to men as a punishment.

Paintings of gladiators were especially popular and had been since the Republican period. Some of these illustrations may even have been the inspiration for some surviving gladiatorial mosaics (the famous Alexander mosaic from Pompeii is thought

━━━━━━━━━━━━━━━━◆━●━◆━━━━━━━━━━━━━━

*Pontarius ('bridge fighter')*
- Armour: shoulderguard
- Special feature: on a wooden platform, armed with a trident and rocks
- Period: Imperial
- Common opponent: *arbelas; essedarius; murmillo; secutor*

━━━━━━━━━━━━━━━━◆━●━◆━━━━━━━━━━━━━━

to have been a copy of a Hellenistic painting). Pliny the Elder tells of some pictures at an exhibition in Rome at the time of Nero:

> A freedman of the same prince, on the occasion of his exhibiting a show of gladiators at Antium, had the public porticos hung, as everybody knows, with paintings, in which were represented genuine portraits of the gladiators and all the other assistants. Indeed, at this place, there has been a very prevailing taste for paintings for many ages past. Gaius Terentius Lucanus was the first who had combats of gladiators painted for public exhibition: in honour of his grandfather, who had adopted him, he provided thirty pairs of gladiators in the Forum, for three consecutive days, and exhibited a painting of their combats in the Grove of Diana. (Pliny, *Natural History* 35.33)

It was, incidentally, a senator by the name of Terentius Lucanus (although not necessarily the same one) who brought the comic playwright Terence to Rome in the middle of the 2nd century BC. A description of such illustrations survives in a poem by Horace:

> How are you less to blame than I, when I admire the combats of Fulvius and Rutuba and Placideianus, with their bended knees,

painted in crayons or charcoal, as if the men were actually engaged, and push and parry, moving their weapons? (Horace, *Satires* 2.7.96–100)

Thus the Roman ambivalence towards gladiators is neatly bracketed by Cicero and Terentius. Indeed, the Romans had a complex set of snobberies that were both class and occupation based, but they left little doubt that gladiators lay right at the bottom of the social ladder. The problem lay in the concept of *infamia*, which was a vague but pernicious notion in Roman society. There were even formal manifestations of this prejudice. By way of example, the *Lex Acilia Repetundarum* of 123 BC ruled that gladiators were perpetually disqualified from the jury set up by that law (which was designed to counter corruption amongst senators). This was the main reason why it was seen as so disgraceful that free men (and most particularly women) should voluntarily perform as gladiators, whilst for an emperor to do so just beggared belief.

The issue of status was the principal reason why emperors who actually fought (rather than just trained) as gladiators were disdained. This of course was most evident with the gladiator emperor himself, Commodus:

> As far as these activities are concerned, however, even if his conduct was hardly becoming for an emperor, he did win the approval of the mob for his courage and his marksmanship. But when he came into the amphitheatre naked, took up arms, and fought as a gladiator, the people saw a disgraceful spectacle, a nobly born emperor of the Romans, whose fathers and forebears had won many victories, not taking the field against barbarians or opponents worthy of the Romans, but disgracing his high position by degrading and disgusting exhibitions. (Herodian 2.15.7)

In his rather extraordinary work of dream interpretation, Artemidorus took what type of gladiator a man dreamed of being and used it to predict what sort of wife he would marry. Beyond the intriguing revelation that men had such dreams in

As was hinted at in the epitaph of Glaucus, gladiators had a special relationship with **Nemesis**, the goddess of divine retribution. Shrines of Nemesis are known in a number of amphitheatres, often set into one side of the arena wall. However, it is clear from surviving inscriptions that not just gladiators revered her, as is attested by an altar found in the nemeseum of the amphitheatre outside the legionary fortress at Chester:

> For the goddess Nemesis, Sextius Marcianus, centurion, after a dream (*RIB* 3149)

Gladiators also felt a close affinity with **Hercules** (which partly explains Commodus' obsession with the hero). When they retired, they often dedicated their weapons to him and a shrine to Hercules was excavated in the amphitheatre in London.

the Roman period, this curious notion seems to provide an even greater subtlety of differentiation between the types of gladiator, in Artemidorus' mind at least, and at a level akin to tea-leaf reading. *Infamia* seems to have been nuanced.

# CHAPTER 7

━●━▬━ ━●━▬━ ━●━▬━ ━●━▬━

# THE END OF THE GLADIATORS

*The race of gladiators has not died: every artist is one.*
*He amuses the public with his afflictions.*

Gustave Flaubert

THE MORALITY OF GLADIATORIAL COMBAT HAD long been discussed by Romans, and whilst most had no problem with the concept, it is clear that even the most learned men had time to consider that there were indeed moral questions to answer. Cicero, one of Rome's greatest legal (and philosophical, or so he liked to think) minds in the Late Republican period, saw a particular nobility in what they did:

> What wounds will the gladiators bear, who are either barbarians, or the very dregs of mankind! How do they, who are trained to it, prefer being wounded to basely avoiding it! How often do they prove that they consider nothing but the giving satisfaction to their masters or to the people! For when covered with wounds, they send to their masters to learn their pleasure: if it is their will, they are ready to lie down and die. What gladiator, of even moderate reputation, ever gave a sigh? who ever turned pale? who ever disgraced himself either in the actual combat, or even when about to die? who that had been defeated ever drew in his neck to avoid the stroke of death? So great is the force of practice, deliberation, and custom! Shall this, then, be done by a Samnite rascal, worthy of his trade; and shall a

man born to glory have so soft a part in his soul as not to be able to fortify it by reason and reflection? The sight of the gladiators' combats is by some looked on as cruel and inhuman, and I do not know, as it is at present managed, but it may be so; but when the guilty fought, we might receive by our ears perhaps (but certainly by our eyes we could not) better training to harden us against pain and death. (Cicero, *Tusculan Disputations* 2.17)

However, as we have seen, Cicero was not above using the term 'gladiator' as a mischievous insult when it suited his purposes. This was particularly so when he felt both the appearance and behaviour of the individual matched those of the stereotypical gladiator, as was the case with Marc Antony. This was all part of the ambiguous position gladiators held in Roman society: to some they were sporting heroes, to others they were the dregs of the social strata.

# Christianity

Christianity was becoming influential within Roman society well before its official adoption under Constantine (AD 306–37). This was particularly true in the Roman army, as is demonstrated by the house church near the fortress at Lajjun in Israel and perhaps in the garrison town of Dura-Europos in Syria, both dating to the first half of the 3rd century AD. Dura even had a small amphitheatre of its own, next to the military compound in the north of the city. The Roman army was becoming Christianised whilst still maintaining an interest in the games.

What is perhaps surprising to a modern reader is that the subsequent adoption of Christianity as the state religion by Constantine did not instantly see the banning of gladiatorial combat. However, this is to misunderstand the context of the times and the everyday brutality with which the inhabitants of the Roman Empire were familiar. The voices raised against the games, which had always been there, became more insistent and

*Retiarius ('net fighter')*
- Armour: shoulderguard
- Special feature: net, trident
- Period: Imperial
- Common opponent: *arbelas; essedarius; murmillo; secutor*

now had scripture to back them up, but as yet they had not been very successful.

In fact, Constantine did produce a rescript (a response for clarification on a specific legal question) in AD 325 related to curtailing deaths in the arena. However, it was not aimed at gladiators as such, but rather at those condemned to the arena (*damnatio ad ludum*) as a method of execution – the same group that made Seneca so uncomfortable. This form of punishment was still going on in AD 315, when the *vicarius* of Africa, one Domitius Celsus, provided a rescript changing the sentence for kidnappers from being condemned to the mines (*damnatio ad metallum*) to being condemned to the games (*damnatio ad ludum*). He specifically ruled that they be handed over to an Imperial *ludus* and that they die without going through gladiatorial training.

In a famous (or perhaps, more correctly, infamous) passage, the 4th-century AD Christian writer Augustine of Hippo tells the story of his student Alypius of Thagaste (who later went on to become a bishop) as a warning against the corrupting influence of the games:

> He, retaining that worldly way which his parents had taught him to follow, had preceded me to Rome in order to study law, and

there he became extraordinarily obsessed with gladiatorial shows. For, being utterly opposed to and detesting such spectacles, he one day happened to meet various friends and fellow-students returning from dinner, and they with a friendly violence led him, vehemently objecting and resisting, into the amphitheatre, on a day of these cruel and deadly shows, as he protested: 'Though you drag me in and keep me there, can you force me to pay attention and watch these shows? So I shall not be there whilst there and will overcome both you and them.' Hearing this, they dragged him on regardless, possibly hoping to see whether he could do as he said. When they had arrived there and had taken their places, the whole place became excited with the inhuman sports. He, however, shutting his eyes, trying to ignore this evil; if only he had shut his ears too! For, when someone fell in combat, a mighty cry from the whole audience stirring him strongly, he, overcome by curiosity, and prepared as it were to despise and overcome it, no matter what it were, opened his eyes, and was struck with a deeper wound in his soul than the other, whom he desired to see, was in his body; and he fell more miserably than the man whose fall had caused the mighty uproar, which entered through his ears, and unlocked his eyes, to make way for the striking and beating down of his soul, which was now bold rather than valiant; and so much the weaker in that it presumed on itself, which ought to have depended on You. For, as soon as he saw blood, he developed a sort of savagery. He did not look away, but stared, drinking in madness unconsciously, and was delighted with the guilty contest, and drunk with the bloody

*Sagittarius ('archer')*
- Armour: unknown
- Special feature: composite bow
- Period: Imperial
- Common opponent: unknown

events. And he was no longer the same as he had been when he came in, but was now one of the crowd and a true companion for those who had brought him in. Need I say more? He looked, shouted, became excited, and took away with him the obsession which would drive him to return, not only with those who first tempted him, but also in fact ahead of them, bringing others with him. (Augustine, *Confessions* 6.8)

## Late instances

One of the most famous depictions of gladiatorial combat – the Borghese mosaic from Torrenova, just outside Rome (see p. 141) – has been dated to the first half of the 4th century AD. From the level of detail it depicts, it seems safe to say that gladiatorial combat with a range of *armaturae* was not only familiar to the artist but in fact acutely observed. Indeed, in AD 337, Constantine received a request from the town of Hispellum in Spain to perform a sacrifice and hold gladiatorial games in his honour. He responded by denying permission for the sacrifice as un-Christian, but allowing the gladiatorial combat. The Church declared that gladiators and *lanistae* could no longer be baptised. Even so, in 354, the annual December games were still held in Rome, according to the Calendar of Philocalus.

The continued existence of gladiators is to some extent confirmed by the fact that, in AD 367, Pope Demasius employed a troop of gladiators in his bodyguard. In 392, Dio Chrystostom mentions gladiatorial performances in Antioch, whilst the local bishop in Apamea (Syria) hired gladiators to help him destroy pagan temples. Nevertheless, it is generally thought that *munera* largely vanished from the East after the middle of the 4th century AD, continuing in just the Western Empire, although even there, Valentinian I (AD 364–75) ended the condemnation of criminals to gladiatorial schools. The Imperial training barracks in Rome are last mentioned in AD 397 and it has been suggested that they may have closed soon after. The historian Ammianus

Marcellinus, writing in the latter part of the 4th century AD on the laziness of the common people, included a list of types of public show when making his point:

> And it has now come to this, that in place of the lively sound of approval from men appointed to applaud, at every public show an actor of afterpieces, a beast-baiter, a charioteer, every kind of player, and the magistrates of higher and lower rank, and even matrons, are greeted with the shout 'You should be these fellows' teachers!' but what they ought to learn no one is able to explain. (Ammianus Marcellinus 28.4.33)

The omission of gladiators may be significant. However, it was not until AD 404 that gladiatorial games were supposedly formally banned by the Emperor Honorius (AD 384–423), although doubt has even been cast over this. The only legislation from Honorius' time dealt with exiling gladiators who moved from training schools to the households of senators, possibly to prevent them being used as armed bodyguards for the nobility. Similarly, there have been claims that a decree of Valentinian III (AD 425–55) in around AD 440 actually brought about the end of gladiatorial combat but the evidence for this is lacking.

Rather than being legislated out of existence, gladiatorial games may just have declined in popularity as tastes changed. Wild beast hunts and chariot racing continued and the latter were still to be found in Constantinople up to the beginning of the 13th century. The 5th-century AD Christian writer Prudentius seems to have had no issues with animal hunts:

> Command that the dead bodies of wretched men be not offered in sacrifice. Let no man fall at Rome that his suffering may give pleasure, nor [the Vestal] Virgins delight their eyes with slaughter upon slaughter. Let the ill-famed arena be content now with wild beasts only, and no more make a sport of murder with blood-stained weapons. (Prudentius, *Against Symmachus* 2.1126–9)

The range of exotic animals declined as Rome's fortunes failed and her empire started to crumble. What was once a sign of the extent of her control now became a warning of its limits. Nevertheless, animal hunts continued with beasts that could be obtained nearer to home. There are records of *venationes* in AD 519 and 523 by the consuls and it is suggested that this was done with the approval of Theodoric. He subsequently wrote to the consul Anicius Maximus deploring the show, whilst conceding that they remained popular with the common people.

Indeed, the one area of gladiatorial combat that seems to have continued into the medieval period, right through to the modern day, is bull fighting, precisely because Christian thinkers were by and large untroubled with the welfare of animals. Roman arenas such as Arles and Nîmes in France are still used for bull fights nowadays (although in Spain open plazas were preferred until comparatively recently). Bull fighting has remained popular from the medieval period onwards in certain selected provincial areas, but now there are indications that it is declining in popularity. A recent poll claimed that only 9.5% of Spaniards paid to visit a bullfight in 2015, placing it tenth behind attending the cinema, monuments, museums, public libraries, football matches, modern music concerts, exhibitions, the theatre and art galleries. The day may soon come when this last vestige of the *munera* has vanished and there are doubtless many who will wonder why it has taken so long. Which brings us right back to the ambivalence of both the Romans and the modern public towards gladiatorial games, that fine balance between horror and fascination that ensures it is now still a topic of conversation.

Perhaps this is also the appropriate point to reflect upon not why gladiators died out, but how they managed to last so long. Societies and their institutions inevitably evolve and the Romans, for all their innate conservatism, were no different. Just as the Roman army at any stage was radically different from what it had been a century before or would be in one hundred years' time, so the institution of gladiatorial combat changed. What is intriguing is how it ceased to evolve under the High and Late Empire, but rather appeared to freeze in the form it had adopted under the early emperors. Why was this? We cannot know for sure, but it seems unlikely that it was down to just one factor and was most likely a result of a combination of circumstances, some of which we may be able to identify, whilst others remain obscure. The formalisation of locations for the games may well have played a significant part, particularly once the Colosseum had been constructed and inaugurated. Once ad hoc venues were no longer needed, the structure itself could become part of the institution. Similarly, the types of gladiator underwent their most active phase of change towards the end of the Republic and the beginning of the Empire. Old types (like the Samnite and Gaul) were dropped and new ones (such as the *retiarius*) adopted. After that, however, there was developmental stagnation that lasted into the Late Roman period, so perhaps it is not surprising that ultimately there was no need for legislation to finish off gladiatorial combat as it had already doomed itself to irrelevance. In which case, the objections of the Christian thinkers may have been symptomatic, rather than a cause, of its end.

# SOURCES

Auguet, R. (1970). *Cruelty and Civilization: The Roman Games*. London, Routledge.

Baker, A. (2002). *The Gladiator: the Secret History of Rome's Warrior Slaves*. Cambridge MA, Da Capo.

Bateman, N. (2000). *Gladiators at the Guildhall: the Story of London's Roman Amphitheatre and Medieval Guildhall*. London, Museum of London Archaeology Service.

Bishop, M. C. (2016). *The Gladius: the Roman Short Sword*. Oxford, Osprey Publishing.

Bishop, M. C. and Coulston, J. C. N. (2006). *Roman Military Equipment from the Punic Wars to the Fall of Rome*. Oxford, Oxbow Books.

Bomgardner, D. L. (2002). *The Story of the Roman Amphitheatre*. London, Routledge.

Christesen, P. & Kyle, D. G. (2013). *Blackwell Companions to the Ancient World: Companion to Sport and Spectacle in Greek and Roman Antiquity*. Chichester, Wiley-Blackwell.

Connolly, P. (2003). *Colosseum: Rome's Arena of Death*. London, BBC Books.

Dodge, H. (2011). *Spectacle in the Roman World*. London, Bristol Classical Press.

Dunkle, R. (2013). *Gladiators. Violence and Spectacle in Ancient Rome*. Abingdon, Routledge.

Epplett, C. (2016). *Gladiators and Beast Hunts. Arena Sports of Ancient Rome*. Barnsley, Pen and Sword.

Futrell, A. (2006). *The Roman Games: a Sourcebook*. Malden MA, Blackwell Pub.

Grant, M. (1971). *Gladiators*. Harmondsworth, Penguin Books.

Hopkins, K. & Beard, M. (2011). *The Colosseum*. London, Profile.

Jacobelli, L. (2006). *Gladiators at Pompeii*. Los Angeles CA, Getty.

Junkelmann, M. (2000). 'Gladiatorial and military equipment and fighting technique: a comparison', *Journal of Roman Military Equipment Studies* 11, 113–17.

Kanz, F. and Grossschmidt, K. (2006). 'Head injuries of Roman gladiators'. *Forensic Science International* 160, 207–16. <http://bit.ly/2sOQ3vL> accessed 19.6.17.

Köhne, E., Ewigleben, C., & Jackson, R. (2000). *Gladiators and Caesars: the Power of Spectacle in Ancient Rome*. Berkeley CA, University of California Press.

Macelduff, S. (n.d.) *Spectacles in the Roman World: A Copyright Free Sourcebook* http://bit.ly/2h9Ikzw

Mannix, D. P. (1960). *Those About to Die*. Panther, London.

Matyszak, P. (2011). *Gladiator: the Roman Fighter's (Unofficial) Manual*. London, Thames & Hudson.

Meijer, F. (2004). *The Gladiators: History's Most Deadly Sport*. London, Souvenir Press.

Nosov, K. (2011). *Gladiator: the Complete Guide to Ancient Rome's Bloody Fighters*. Guilford, Conn, Lyons Press.

Scarborough, J. (1971) 'Galen and the Gladiators'. *Episteme* 5, 98–11. <http://bit.ly/2rw9oxQ> accessed 19.6.17.

Shadrake, S. (2005). *The World of the Gladiator*. Stroud, Tempus.

Shaw, B. D. (2001). *Spartacus and the Slave Wars: A Brief History with Documents*. New York NY and Boston MA, Bedford.

Strauss, B. (2010). *The Spartacus War*. London, Phoenix.

Wiedemann, T. (1992). *Emperors and Gladiators*. London, Routledge.

Winkler, M. M. (2004). *Gladiator: Film and History*. Oxford, Blackwell.

# NOTE ON TRANSLATIONS

WITH THE EXCEPTION OF THE QUOTATION from Vegetius and most of the inscriptions, which are my own translations, all of the texts cited here are derived from public domain works freely available on the internet. These are usually old Loeb texts, many of which have been transcribed through the efforts of Bill Thayer, who deserves acknowledgement for his stalwart contribution to the dissemination of valuable source material. In one or two places I have tweaked the English to render the text less dated. Readers wishing to find links for all of the sources cited here, both textual and visual, should visit http://tinyurl.com/GladiatorsFTTD for more information.

# INDEX

ALSO AVAILABLE

# GREEK WARRIORS

HOPLITES AND HEROES

*CAROLYN WILLEKES*

Thermopylae, Marathon: though fought 2,500 years ago in ancient Greece, the names of these battles are more familiar to many than battles fought in the last half-century, but our concept of the men who fought in these battles may be more a product of Hollywood than Greece. Shaped by the landscape in which they fought, the warriors of ancient Greece were mainly heavy infantry. While Bronze Age Greeks fought as individuals, for personal glory, the soldiers of the Classical city states fought as hoplites, armed with long spears and large shields, in an organised formation called the phalanx. This book sketches the change from heroic to hoplite warfare, and discusses the equipment and training of both the citizen soldiers of most Greek cities, and the professional soldiers of Sparta.

Carolyn Willekes is a lecturer based at the University of Calgary. She specializes in Greek history and archaeology, especially the late Classical and Hellenistic periods, with a particular interest in cavalry and horse culture.

ISBN 9781612005157 • £7.99 • $12.95